C++ PROGRAMMING

Step-by-Step Instructions for Creating a Robust Program from Scratch (Computer Programming Crash Course 2022)

Troy Carter

TABLE OF CONTENTS

INTRODUCTION

This book is good for people who are new to programming and for people who want to learn more about backend programming. Even though C++ is sometimes seen as a ghost from the past, the language is still alive and well, and it still plays a big role in some of the most important technologies we use today. In the past, it has been one of the most important languages in the world. It isn't going anywhere, and learning it will open up your world.

C++ is often used as a backend language for big data because it takes very little time to process the data. You'll soon see why companies like Spotify, Adobe, YouTube, and Amazon use C++ to run their backends, and you'll start to see why soon enough.

C++ is also used to make powerful game engines. Gamming engines let programmers make a game without having to write everything from scratch. They also make it easier to show the content in a game. A game engine that runs on C++ is Unity Game Engine or Unreal Engine.

This is why C++ is a beautiful and efficient language: it has a good power-to-hardware ratio. It uses very little hardware for the power it gives us. They love it because they learned how to do it. This is why.

In this book we will cover the following topics:

- Programming terminology and principles in programming
- Setting up a C++ environment

- Getting Started: Syntax, Data Types, and Variables
- Power of C++: Operations, Loops, Switches, and DecisionMaking
- Creating custom functions in C++

You will also find a useful glossary at the end so that you can use thebook as a reference once you get cracking.

CHAPTER 1:

SETTING UP A C++ DEVELOPMENT ENVIRONMENT

At its most basic, programming is writing a list of instructions in code that the machine can understand. The code resides in executables files. These files come with file extensions that tell a compiler what language is in the file. These extensions are the suffixes you often see at the end of the file, like ".js". ".cpp" or ".hpp".

To write code and save it in an executable file you need the followingthings:

A **text editor**: this will allow you to write and edit the code.

A **language compiler**: This program takes the code you have written and translates it into machine language that your computer can understand and follow.

All programming languages work like this except HTML, CSS, and JavaScript - these programs are interpreted and executed by the browser ("Introduction," n.d.). This means browser languages like JavaScript are software-based, while C++ is compiled and then run directly on your machine, not in a software environment.

This means C++ is an assembly language. **Assembly languages** are low-level programming languages that need a compiler so they can run on a machine (Lithmee, 2018). In this context, the word low- level does not carry a bad connotation; it is descriptive, meaning thatthe language is closer to the machine or just a step away from it.

As you can probably guess, C++ is a general-purpose language that can run almost anywhere. This means it can be assembled and compiled in several different ways. This will largely depend on your operating system and the creation utilities you are using.

Our C++ exercises will be compiled on an online IDE. IDE stands for **Integrated Development Environment** and it is used to edit and compile code. I bet that description sounds familiar. Yes, an IDE isan example of a text editor, but unlike a plain text editor, it has extra features that are important to the programming process. An IDE can do things like compile code, debug code, highlight code, warn you of syntax errors, and more.

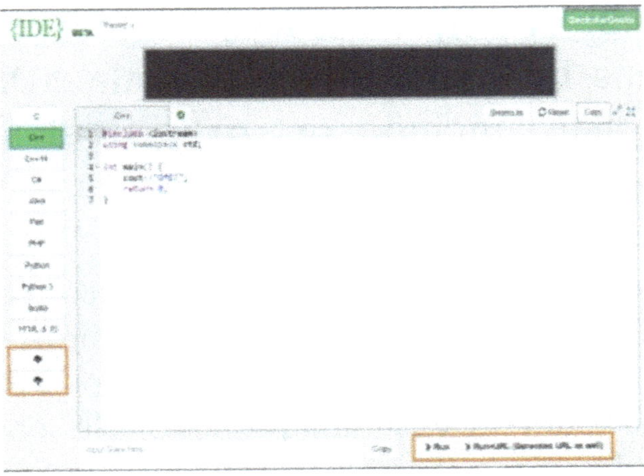

In this book, we will use a Geeks for Geeks web-based IDE, but you should learn to set up a local IDE. For the majority of your programming career, that is where you will be working. Plus, you cancustomize the IDE to fit your needs and spruce up your code.

Setting up Your Text Editor

IDE environments that are focused on programming always have to have a text editor and a compiler within them. Non-IDE environments separate compilers and plain text editors. The text editor serves as a programming interface in non-IDE setups; this simply means the text editor will be the place you tinker with the code.

> **Note:** If you have a Linux, you will already have a text editor as Linux is a console-based environment. Console-based environments use a **command-line interface (CLI),** where you interact with programs by issuing lines of code. IDE for Linux may include a **graphical user**

When looking for a text editor, you need one with syntax highlighting and indenting as all programming languages follow their syntax. This is because you want to be able to read your code easily and you want collaborators to be able to do so, too. These text editors help by improving readability. This is especially important because coding is no longer and has never been a solitary task. There is no one-man genius like in the movies.

Github and Pastebin are code aggregators that have syntax highlighting add-ons enabled. Github will allow you to host your entire project on their site, while Pastebin only allows code snippets. On these platforms, you can save code in a variety of languages.

They are very useful to programmers because they allow programmers to share code, collaborate, test, and so forth. Learning how to deploy a project to Github is one of the most important things in programming because it has become so standardized. So, maintaining a Github profile has also become important, as it holds all the projects you are working on, have worked on, and your activity (Peshev, 2017). To a potential employer or collaborator, this information is invaluable.

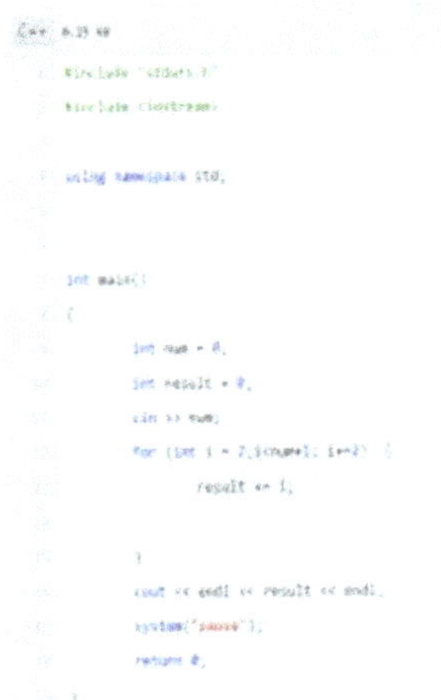

C++ Code Syntax Example

This is a screenshot from Paste Bin with syntax highlighting enabled ("C++ Code," 2015). Syntax highlighting and tabbed spacing help with making the code more comprehensible. All text editors with syntax highlighting will use this scheme: libraries in green, and functions, data types, and data in blue. Strings will show up as red.

When you are working locally you will not have luxuries like these readily available. The first text editor you will find on your system if you are using windows is Notepad. Wordpad is another one that has more GUI features. What you will notice as you open these programs is how plain and boring they are. They are like Word but worse, because they shouldn't be simple word processors if writing efficient, elegant code is important to us. Their word processor-like aspects make them more suitable for writing words in them, notcode, although you can code in them.

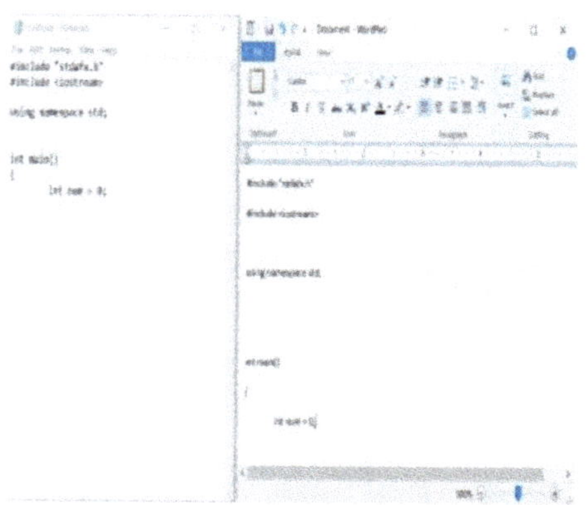

Side-by-side comparison of Windows' Notepad utility and Wordpad utility

This is a screenshot that features two of Windows' built-in utilities, Notepad on the left and Wordpad on the right. Wordpad has more Microsoft suite GUI features that may be more recognizable to you,including Microsoft's quick access bar located above the highlighted "File" tab. Notepad is very bare-bones in comparison. Both utilities, unlike word processors, allow you to save in different file extensions. However, Wordpad is more similar to a word processor than Notepad, saving files in rich text format (.rtf). Wordpad will warn you that you will lose formatting if you save in anextension other than rich text format.

What makes Notepad and Wordpad unique is that they can savefiles in a variety of file extensions, while word processors cannot. File extensions are important because they tell the compiler how to interpret what is written in the file, and that leads to the machine having a set of instructions it can understand and execute.

Despite their abilities, these two programs lack crucial text editor features like syntax highlighting. You might think this is no big deal, but it is; the same words in code can mean different things because of how and when they appear, so highlighting helps us distinguish what they refer to. So if everything is plain, black and white, you have to work harder to figure out what a piece of code refers to. It sounds complex now, but once you code this will become obvious and necessary.

Notepad++, not to be confused with Windows 'Notepad, has highlighting features but you will have to activate them like so:

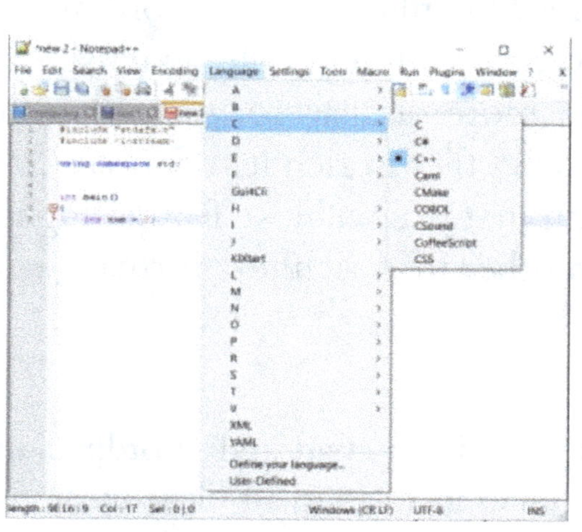

Screenshot of Notepad ++ with C++ Syntax

Notepad ++ is free and, as the name suggests, was programmed inC++. This screenshot illustrates how to enable language syntax. C++ syntax can specifically be enabled by going to language >"C"

> and navigating to C++. Notepad++ is only available on the Windows platform (Orin, n.d.).

Bluefish is a more advanced text editor that comes with more features ("Bluefish Editor: Features," n.d.). Unlike Notepad++, Bluefish is available on multiple platforms other than Windows. But I would not recommend Bluefish for beginners because it has a lot of features that can be overwhelming to a complete beginner. If you arenot new to programming you can go give it a shot; you will find it has many of the GUI features typical of an IDE text editor.

Once in the text editor, you must select a compiler. Now let me showyou how you would set up your local environment on three platforms: Windows, Linux, and Mac.

Windows IDE Installation and Setup

All you need to do is to install an IDE. Just remember that it has to have a text editor and a compiler within it. **Code::Blocks** is a useful, open-source IDE made for C++ and it easily fits with a variety of compilers including Microsoft's Visual C++. Installing Code::Block is easy. You just have to go to their downloads page at http://www.codeblocks.org/downloads/26 and select the latest version.

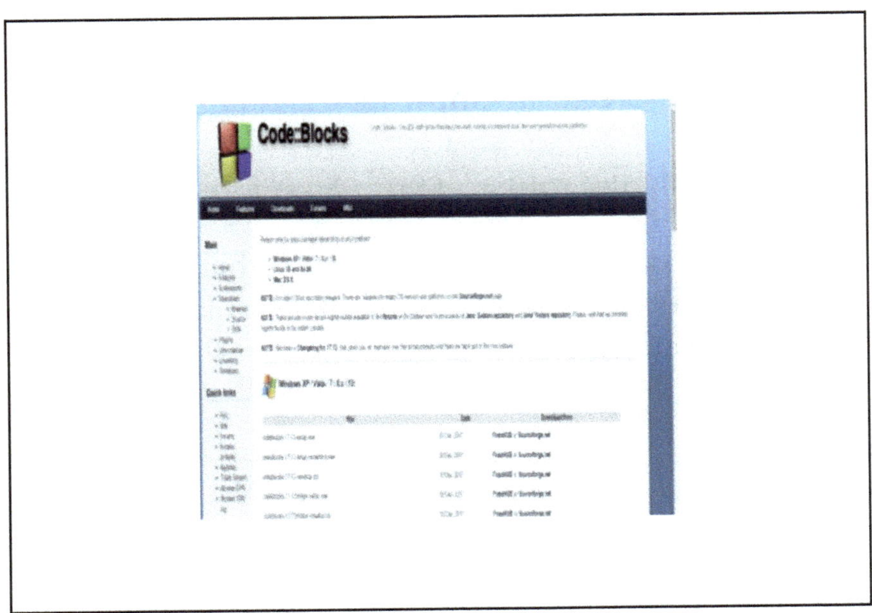

Code::Blocks Download Page

As of this writing, Code::Blocks has version 20.03 for Windows and Linux distributions. The page also includes helpful notes for installation.

Once the program is installed, you are set. You can use it to write C++ programs. To do so you have to follow three steps: creating a file, building the program, and running the program.

Creating a new file is a bit more nuanced. Here is what you have to do:

Go to File > New

Select "Create an empty file" and input your code

Save the file with a ".cpp" extension

And, needless to say, you have to build a program before you can run it. You can do this by going to Build > "Build and Run" in the menu.

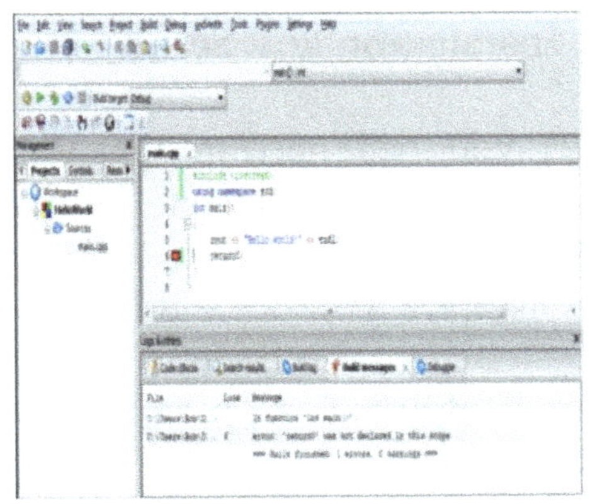

Screenshot of "Hello World" in Code::Blocks

This is a live screenshot of our "Hello World" program in code blocks. After this program is run, an error shows up in the Build Messages of the code. Code::Blocks highlights the error on line 6. Given your knowledge of C++ syntax from the earlier section, you should see how to repair the code. How can we repair the code?

Hint: Data and functions are supposed to show up in blue.

By the way, this program is very lightweight for the amount of work it allows you to do. Code::Block is available on Windows and Linux, but there is no Mac version.

Mac OS IDE Installation and Setup

For Mac, you will need to get **Xcode**. It is a free IDE softwaredevelopment suite for macOS. You can get it on the Mac App Store. Xcode supports a variety of other languages like Java, Python, and Ruby.

It is geared toward developing software for macOS operating systems; this can be for the tvOS for AppleTV, watchOS for Apple watches, and the iPadOS for iPad tablets ("What's New in Xcode 9," n.d.). Xcode offers a variety of **software development kits** (SDKs) for different MacOS platforms to help programmers through Apple's proprietary programming schemes. SDKs are a set of tools, provided by hardware and software vendors, used for developing applications for specific platforms ("What's New in Xcode 9," n.d.). SDKs allow developers to be fully integrated within a development community, like Apple's or Android's.

Mac uses proprietary compilers that will only work with Xcode, so if you are on Mac you have little choice but to develop with C++ using Xcode. You can download and install Xcode by following this link:

https://apps.apple.com/us/app/xcode/id49779983 5?mt=12

Once the file is downloaded and installed, open Xcode and click on the "Create a new Xcode Project" icon. Then select "New Project" in the initial window.

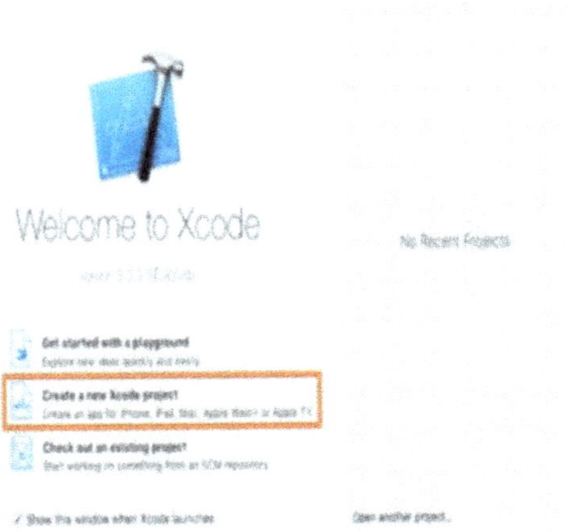

Initial Screen for Xcode: Select a new project

These screenshots feature an Xcode build from version 8.3.3 (Patel, 2017). Therefore, our examples might look different from a more up-to-date build. As of this writing, the most current version is 12.1, which mostly includes updates to the various macOS platform SDKs (" Xcode," n.d.). Despite these differences, these screenshots will still help you orient yourself in the more current build. Our instruction will still yield results.

After you do this, a prompt window will appear that will ask you to choose a template. This window will guide you through the rest of the setup. Select the macOS sections and go to the Application section; in there, choose the Command Line Tool.

It looks something like this:

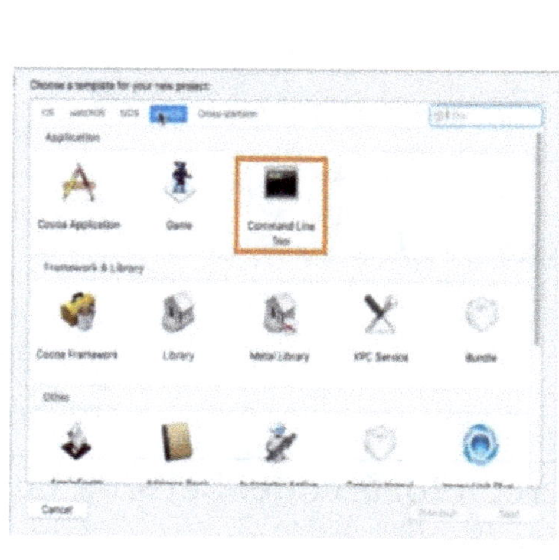

1. Project Selection Screen: macOS > Application > CommandLine Tool

Xcode has many built-in code utilities for running programs onvarious Apple platforms. Therefore, to run a test program you would have to select macOS for it to run on your program. Further,

to access assembly language software development needed for C++, you would have to use Xcode's command-line tool. This command-line tool can handle Objective-C and C languages as well.

After you select a template, the guide will present options for the command-line tool. Here, you can name the project, add your organization's name, use a bundle identifier, and select a programming language.

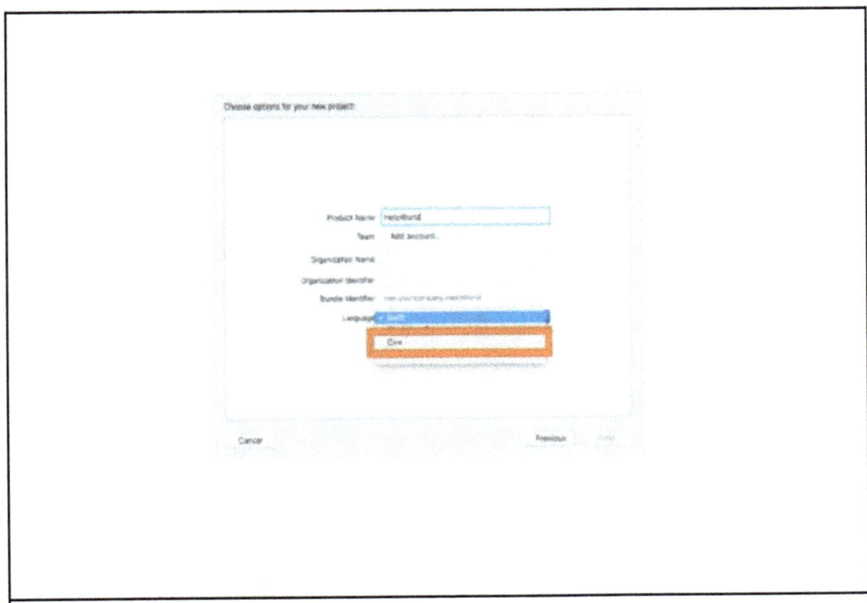

2. Command Line Tool Options: Language > Select C++

Xcode's command-line tool can handle Microsoft's proprietary languages like Swift. This program can run alongside C-basedlanguages in Mac compilers, including C++. Swift is selected by default.

In the same window, you will be required to add an organization identifier. Remember that Xcode's command-line tool is a programming template for proprietary macOS operating systems, so the organization identifier is used to create a unique idea for your program in Apple databases:

the Apple Developer Website and

iCloud Container, iTunes connect portal in the Appstore. This will streamline your app into a proprietary macOS framework.

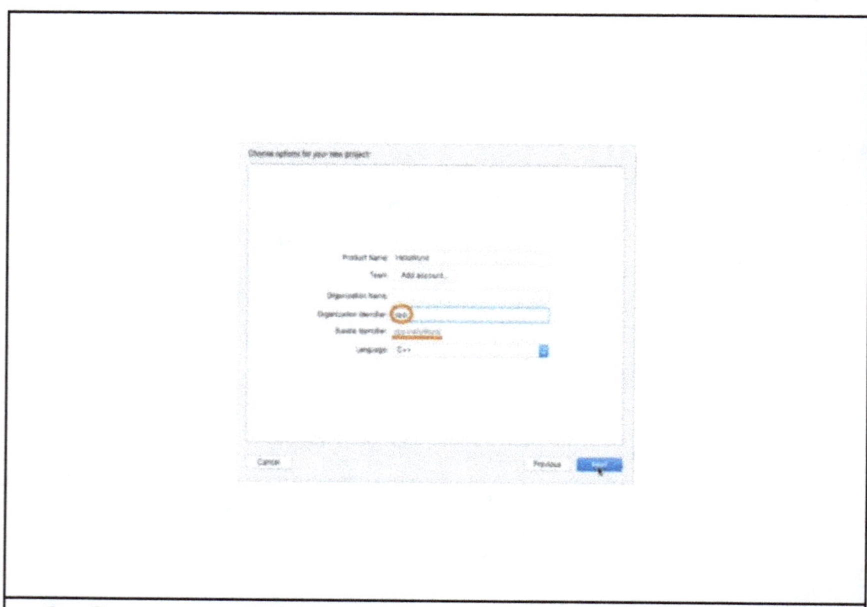

3. Command Line Tool Options: Organization Identifier > "cpp"

The organization's identifier is a naming convention that helps programmers integrate their projects into Apple's proprietary software development scheme. Here, we are using "cpp" as our identifier, which generates "cpp.HelloWorld" as our bundle identifier. Once we indicate an identifier, the guide allows us to proceed to thenext step.

Now, save your project in a directory of your choice. On the left-handside pane, Xcode will be able to open the file. You will have to selectmain.cpp to access the global C++ file for your program in Xcode. If you so desire, you can upload cpp files into the directory, and edit them.

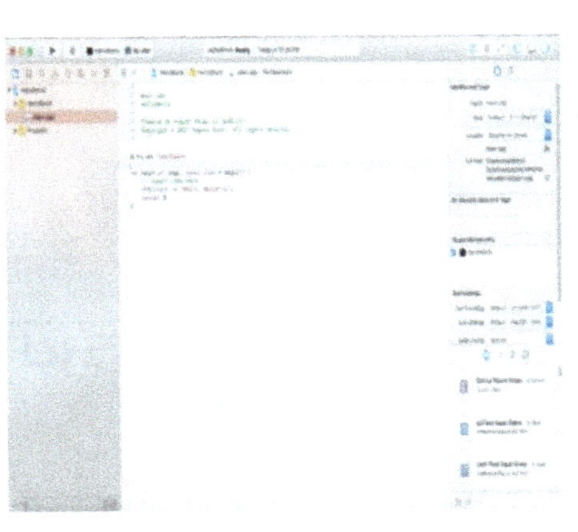

3. Xcode Command Line Tool: "main.cpp"

This screenshot features the IDE style Xcode Command Line Tool workspace. It has the **main.cpp** opened in the text editor (Patel, 2017).

Once you have written some code and you want to run it, you select Product and click on Run. Also, you can run and build the programby selecting the button.

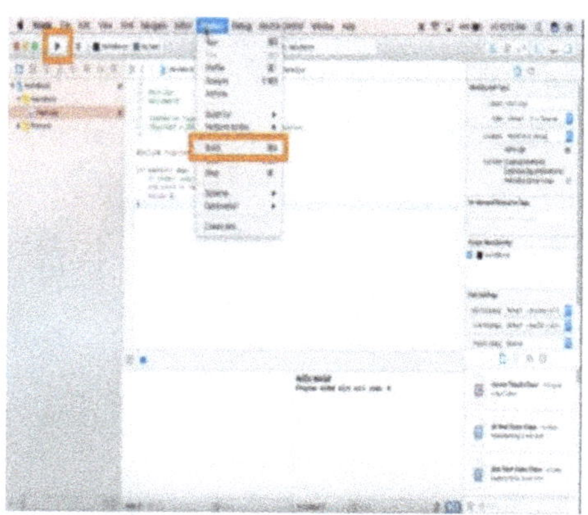

4. Xcode Command Line Tool: "Hello World" Build and Run

Similar to the Code::Blocks IDE, you will also have to build and then run your program. This screenshot also features the results of "Hello World" and the return value (Patel, 2017).

If you are a programmer who sees themselves working with Apple devices, working and practicing in Xcode is a good investment. For instance, Apple has a healthy share of the market in a wide variety ofconsumer goods and services like streaming services and devices. With that said, you should keep in mind that C++ is used mostly as aserver-side language. Server-side programming is code that controlshow content is delivered to a dynamic website like YouTube. Most server-side programming is done on Linux machines.

Linux Compiler Installation

Linux is a console-based operation system, so it does not need a text editor. Instead, we will focus on installing and setting up a programming compiler. Mac and Windows automatically initialize a compiler within the IDE, but in Linux, a more hands-on approach is required. You will be required to execute a backend initialization. It might seem like a lot of work, but in the great scheme of things, it allows those working with Linux to have full control of the development procedure and unlock more computing power.

Because Linux is an operating system that uses a console interface, it will be strange to beginners or anyone who is used to Windows or Mac. This is because users are often used to a GUI. The GUI- lessness of Linux allows more computing power to be freed for programming – a GUI takes some computing power to produce and maintain. This is why many servers and other programming environments have console interfaces. Also, many of them use **Linux distributions**.

A Linux distribution (distro) is an operating system made from Linux kernel-based software collection and package management system for installing additional software.

The following are instructions for installing and initializing a compiler. This will be for Ubuntu, a popular Linux distro for beginners. These installations will be similar in any Linux distro you will be using.

Note: There are many distributions of Linux that provide a GUI based desktop experience that many users love. Most of these are open-source and free to download and install. You can explore thesedistros and create console interfaces to practice on. One free distro to consider is **CentOS**, which is based on Red Hat for server management ("Centos-faq | Open Source Community," n.d.). **Red Hat Enterprise Linux (RHEL)** is used in many server management setups and is not free. However, CentOS uses many of its components and is an excellent distro for preparing to work in Red Hat environments.

In this example, we will use the **GNU Collection Compiler** on Linux. The GNU Collection Compiler is a Linux-based compiler that supports C++ and other various languages like Fortran, Ada, and Java ("GCC 7 Release Series—Changes, New Features, and Fixes

—GNU Project—Free Software Foundation (FSF)," n.d.). To install GNU GCC, follow these steps:

In the console, enter the following commands:

Check first if there is a version already installed on your machine by entering this command: gcc –v

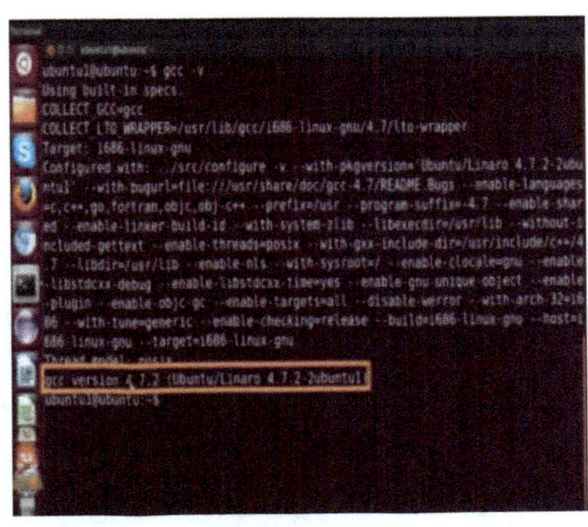

A.   Check for GNU GCC in

Ubuntu Console

You should check your system for a copy of the GCC. This screenshot features a system with GCC already installed (Patel, 2014). After using the command, if there is no copy of GCC in your system, it will be missing this line. If there is a copy, it will have a similar line. Most likely, your version will be more recent.

The following commands will install GCC on your system (Agarwal, 2017b):

sudo apt-get update

sudo apt-get install GCC

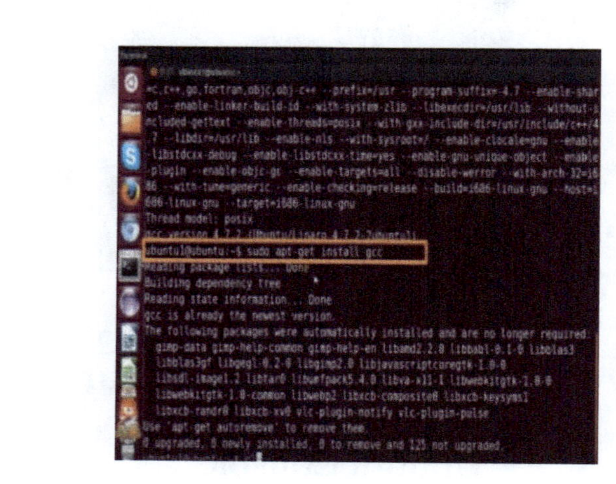

A.   Install GNU GCC in

Ubuntu Console

In the screenshot, a GNC GCC is already present. Running the highlighted command will install the GNU GCC on your system if it isn't there (Patel, 2014). The console will prompt you to type "Y" for it to begin the installation. You also are offered package management features like the ability of the terminal to inform you of outdated or unnecessary packages. It will also suggest commands that will make your system more efficient. This explains the popularity of Linux with programmers; although wordy, it allows them to troubleshoot with ease, gives them more control, and it is easy to navigate when compared to GUIs. This is because programmers are more likely to remember a line of code thanwhere something resides in the GUI.

The following command will install all the libraries required tocompile code and eventually run C++:

sudo apt-get install build-essential

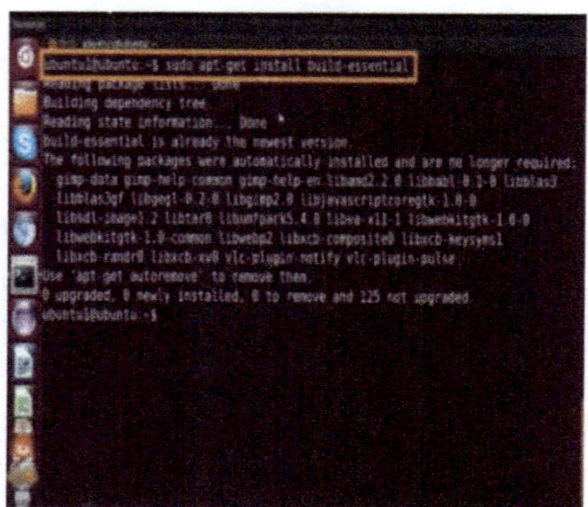

A.   Install GNU GCC in

Ubuntu Console

This screenshot shows a system with the build-essential libraries installed and inputting the highlighted installation command (Patel, 2014). Just as with installing the GCC, after using the commandand finding there is no copy of the build-essential libraries in your system, it will prompt you to install. Type in "Y" and the terminal willinstall libraries.

Check the installation with the following command:g++ --version

If all went well it will tell you what version of GCC is installed.

Because Linux has a built-in text editor you will have to use thefollowing command to access the GUI for the text editor:

gedit

You will be free to write your program as you see fit. Remember to save the programs with the ".cpp" extension so that they will be compiled correctly.

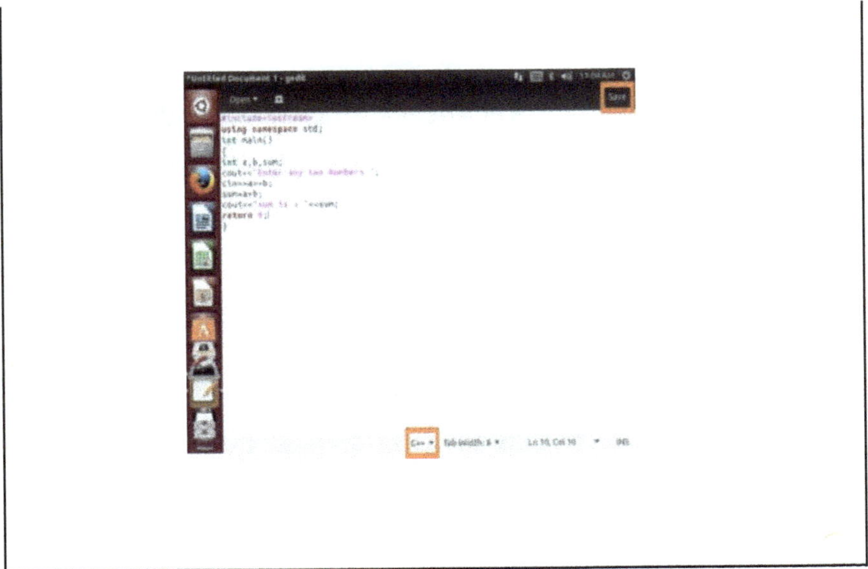

Gedit in Ubuntu

This screenshot features Linux's built-in text-editor, Gedit ([Running C, C++ Programs in Linux] Ubuntu 16.04 (Ubuntu Tutorial for Beginners), n.d.). Gedit is a Linux programming text editor utility that has syntax highlighting and tabbed spacing features for a diverse array of programming languages. Be sure to have "C++" selected from the highlighted dropdown menu. You can save your program file in the GUI by clicking the "save" button. Be sure to list which directory you have your file saved, as you will have to point the compiler to that directory to compile and run the code.

To test and run your code you must follow these instructions:

Lead the terminal to the files directory

To do this use this command. Enter it in the directory repeatedly until the .cpp file is revealed.

ls

Compile and test the program file Use these commands to do so:

g ++- otest[filename].cpp

If there are any errors this command will tell you which line contains the error just like you would expect from an IDE. Then you can open the program file through "gedit [filename.cpp]" and fix the line of code.

Run the program file

The compiler will create an executable file called "test" that will run the program. You can execute it by entering ". /test" in the terminal.

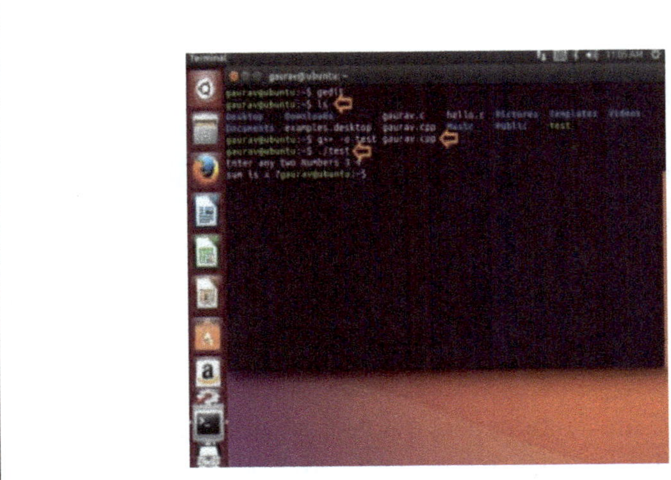

Testing, Compiling and Running a .cpp file in Ubuntu

This screenshot features the terminal testing, compiling, and running the example code written in gedit ([Running C, C++ Programs in Linux] Ubuntu 16.04 (Ubuntu Tutorial for Beginners), n.d.).

Linux distros are verbose console-based systems and most of them can handle programming in any language through the terminal. Learning to work in the Linux environment is beneficial as it exposes you to server-side programming.

Note: The process for installing GCC and compiling on CentOs is similar. To install, you instead use "

yumgroupinstall"DevelopmentTools

.

This command automatically installs the needed libraries as well. The steps forcomposing, compiling, testing, and running the program are all the same.

Creating your own programming environment helps prepare you for real-world scenarios in a way that online coding spaces cannot. In this book, we will be using an online IDE. This is because everyone will have the same learning environment with standardized outputs and interfaces. It simplifies things.

CHAPTER 2:

BASICS OF C++, PRINCIPLESOF PROGRAMMING

Like any other language, programming languages have a structure, syntax, and set of rules that make them easy to learn and use. In order to be a good person, you need to know the words of another language. Knowing how to use them and how they work in that language is an important part of communicating well in that language. They all work the same way, but the communication they care about is between humans and machines. Even though machines aren't as smart or capable as we are today, there is still so much they can learn that we don't understand. They can do this at a rate and in a way that isn't possible for us. All programming is a set of steps. These can be rules, actions you want the machine to do, or something else. In other words, we are able to communicate with each other because we follow the rules of a programming language.

Programming rules, or syntax, are a set of symbols used to communicate things like functions and variables in a program. These symbols are called delimiters. So, how a code looks is important to the compiler. It tells them what instructions to give to a machine.

Keep these things in mind before we start: C++ is not as easy to understand as Python or other high-level programming languages. High-level languages, like JS, Python, and C#, are made this way because it makes them easier to read and manage. This is why they are made this way. C++, even though it is this way, is easier for machines to understand because it isn't so abstracted. This is why. This is why when you work with C++, you only need a compiler and a text editor, but languages like Python need their own environments set up.

Principles of Programming

C++ has many ways of completing the same task. Just like with human languages, there are many ways of saying the same thing, but some ways are best suited for certain occasions and somearen't. C++ is the same way; some methods are great because they reduce program overhead. Many developers will want that because it increases the performance of the entire application, and that is the first principle of programming: complete a task with the least amount of functions as possible. Do not make things more complicated than they need to be. In most cases, this means using a loop or a switch statement in a frugal way.

The best way to do this is by understanding the nature of the problem first and how best to implement the solution. In other words,you will need to write an algorithm – a list of instructions that you want the machine to follow to fix the problem.

Your designs should always begin with the thing you want the program to do. This will also include your algorithm, or at least the problem that your algorithm will fix. The algorithm will always look something like this:

Input: data coming, where applicable

Processing: operations performed on the data anddeclaration of variables

Output: the results, or the action you want performed.

Here is a verbose example of a C++ program for

displaying "Hello World". This is to illustrate how C++ programs are composed:

// Simple C++ program to display "Hello World"

// Header file for input output functions #include<iostream>

using namespace std;

// main function -

// where the execution of program beginsint main()

{

// prints hello world cout<<"Hello World";return 0;

}

Here is the structure:

Call header file for input and output functions

Call the main function where the execution happens

Print "Hello World"

Terminating statement that indicates the state of themachine

We can see how verbose C++ is, because most of the steps regard the backend aspects of C++ that are needed to execute the code, such as calling the library files. Your algorithms don't need to be this detailed most of the time.

Despite being simple, this algorithm illustrates how developers take tasks and translate them into code. In the next chapter, we will use this algorithm to write our program.

As you have noticed in the example, there are comments in the codethat explain what each part of the code does. These comments are preceded by "//". The compiler will not read any lines of code preceded by // because they don't do anything but help other people working on the code read what the code does. It is good practice to include comments in your code so people know what each line of code does.

Overview of the C++ Syntax

We have talked about the importance of syntax for the compiler, but itis also important to understand the syntax of a programming language because it will allow you to debug the code. Just like with human languages, if you know the rules of a language you can correct yourself easily when you make mistakes. **Debugging** is the process of finding and removing errors and abnormalities in the code, also known as "bugs" ("What is Debugging?" n.d.). It is a process of correction.

IDEs have debugging tools that highlight where errors occur in the code, but these features aren't always reliable. For instance, leavingout a semicolon to terminate a line of code is a common error, but the debugger will highlight the error in the (.h) file instead of the code where the mistake happens in the program file (.cpp). Most debuggers are not intelligent enough to detect an absence of something and will throw the verbose error that the compiler gives when the unterminated line violates a rule in the library. However, a programmer will pick up the error simply when they notice the red semicolon line delimiter is missing from one of the lines.

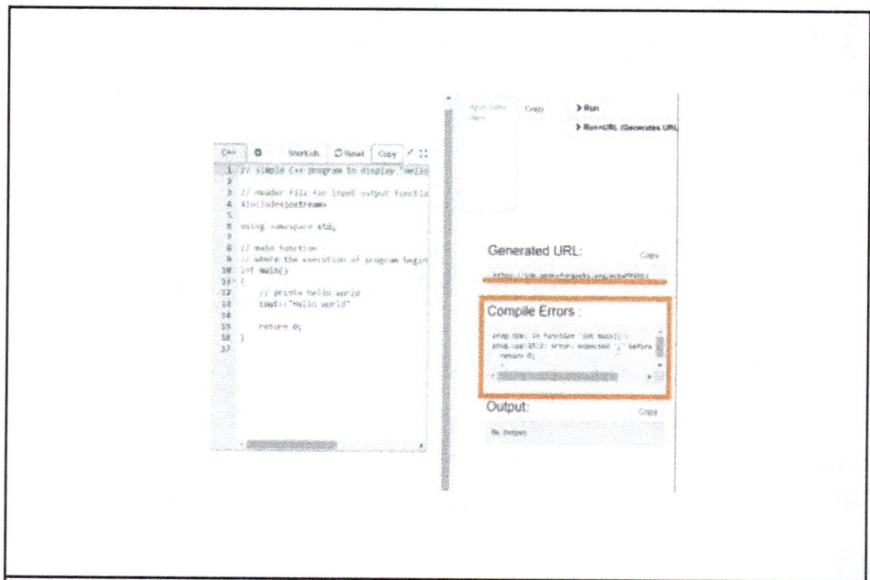

"Hello World" program in GeeksforGeeks IDE without a line delimiter

This screenshot features "Hello World" with a missing delimiter. Immediately you will notice that the IDE has different syntax highlighting for C++ than the programming environments we explored in the previous chapter. Syntax can vary from platform to platform. This is why we are standardizing the process with GeeksforGeeks IDE. In our chosen IDE, semicolons are not highlighted. However, theIDE can make up for this by recognizing and annotating missingsemicolons, as highlighted in the screenshot. You can practice and explore this program by going to its generated URL: https://ide.geeksforgeeks.org/mzbuPP46Sl.

It is easy to see this when the code is small, but when working on a larger project the task can be difficult. I have heard of programmerswho spend a week and or more trying to find or fix a line in their code only to discover it is something very minuscule like a missing letter or mismatch in case. To make debugging easier, it is advised that you separate code into smaller modules ("What is Debugging?" n.d.). Manyerrors can be found and easily dealt with in this way.

Let us look at the "Hello World" program and study its syntax in detail. While syntax highlighting may vary across different platforms, these aspects of code are consistently highlighted on all platforms.

Comments: As I said, these are the lines of code that the compiler will ignore. They are used to annotate code and leave helpful explanations for other programmers. This is great because normally when we code we collaborate with others. It advised that you leave comments in your algorithm to simplify it for others. In most platforms comments will be highlighted green.

Comments are always preceded with (//).

Header File Library: Lines that start with (#) are used by the compiler to call library functions. These lines are very essential, so they appear in every program. In the "Hello World" example we call a library that is used to manage strings. These lines of code will be highlighted in different colors across different platforms. In GeeksforGeeks the coloris purple.

Statements: Statements describe the beginning of a line of code with instructions that the compiler recognizes. This includes declaration handling instructions, like *"using..."* or *"return..."* in our Hello World program. They are also highlighted differently across multiple platforms. On GeeksForGeeks they are highlighted purple.

Functions: This is code that encapsulates instructions. It may take inputs and output a result. Every function is written like this: "[*function_name*] () "followed by curly braces {}. Anything in the curly braces is the set of instructions that will be executed. In our example, *main()* is the function that initiates the instructions that

Note: Recalling our discussion about algorithms from the previous section, your algorithm will mainly describe what instructions occur within the curly brackets of intmain(). More detailed algorithms may explain the sorts of data types needed for

will output "Hello World" with cout<<. In a ".cpp"

program, *int main* () must always appear for the program to **function.**

Data: These are variables and other kinds of data functions and statements. In the GeeksforGeeks IDE, they are highlighted blue.

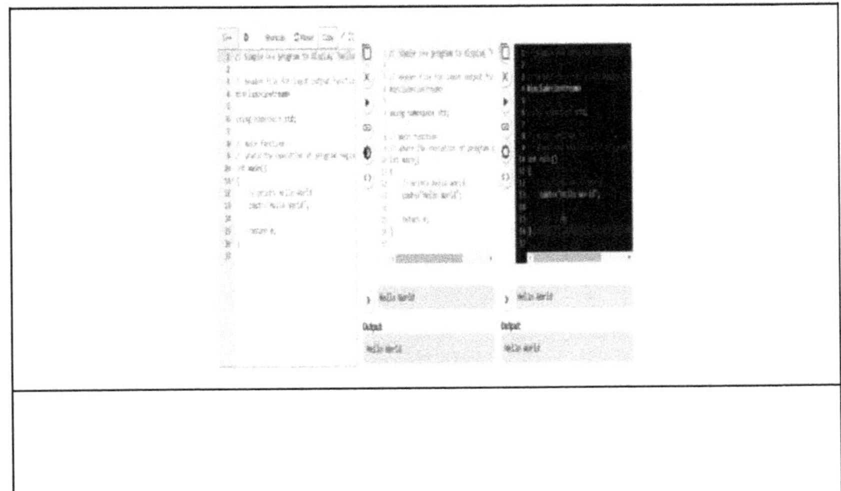

This screenshot features a successful run of "Hello World" with the memory used to run the program. This IDE has light syntax highlighting, focusing mainly on comments, statements, and operand data. Compared to GeeksforGeeks' embedded code in their articles, their embedded code is much more detailed ("Writing first C++ program," 2017). The two screenshots on the right feature the "light- mode" and "dark-mode" views of the same code embedded in their articles. These views are more detailed, highlighting comments, functions, and distinguishing different statements. For example, data types such as

```
int
```

are distinguished with a different color from other statements such as

```
usingnamespace
```

. Also the embedded views, unlike the IDE, distinguish strings from other data. This is a perfect example of how syntax highlighting can vary across different platforms.

Earlier we saw a Code::Block example with an error in it. Below is the very same code next to one that is corrected. Immediately you can begin to appreciate the syntax and what went wrong in the Code::Blockexample.

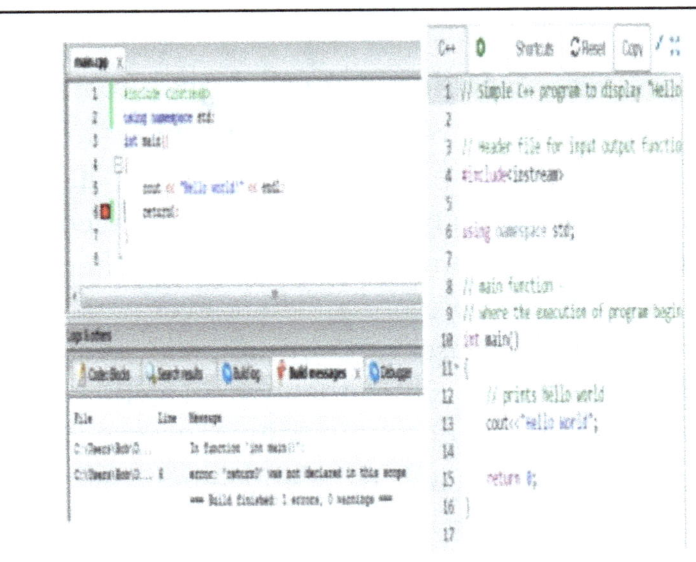

parison of **"Hello World"** in **Code::Blocks**

sforGeeks IDE

screenshot features a side-by-side comparison of previousexample, "Hello World" in Code::Blocks

I will admit that it is not as impressive in a few code lines like this, but being able to notice errors and explain them is one of the most important skills for programmers. At this point you should not worry much about being able to do this. The more you code and learn, the better equipped you will be to notice and fix errors. Software and web development are industries with a high failure rate because of this. To succeed as a developer you need to solve problems quickly, find bugs more efficiently, and fix them. This also applies on the administrative side, because being able to find, fix, and explain bugs is a large part of desk service level agreements.

In tech, **Service Level Agreements** (SLAs) are agreements betweena service provider and a client. They agree upon aspects of the service, like support, quality, availability, and responsibilities (Wieder, Butler, Theilmann, & Yahyapour, 2011). Comprehensive SLAs offer a debugging debriefing, where every error is logged and listed with its cause, workaround, and solution. This is the best way to do it intechnology management firms and development stages. However, administrators have more resources to dedicate to debugging thandevelopers themselves. They are compensated at a higher rate as well. For instance, web developers make approximately $60,000 ayear in the US; web administrators, those in charge of SLAs, make about 1/3 more at $90,000 a year ("15-1199.03—Web Administrators," n.d.). This level of expertise is valuable because it understands howthe compiler translates C++.

First Program: Output and Basic Strings

"Hello World" is every programming language's beginner project; itsaim is to show the learner the basic syntax of the program and how it functions. As you learn more languages you will write many "Hello World" programs. In the previous section, we used it to explore topics like algorithms, syntax, and C++ programming environments. In this section we will go further: we will manipulate the code.

C++ uses the **cout** object from the *iostream* library. An object is a method that a computer uses to manage data. In our example, *cout*was used to tell the compiler to print "Hello World with the >> operator. Don't freak out; we will discuss operators and objects inlater chapters. For now, it's enough to understand that the compiler reads **cout** as specific instructions because that instruction is definedin the *iostream* library that we declared.

Now, let's look at "Hello World" and the cout object by changing the print out. Find the original code here so you can use it as a reference:

https://ide.geeksforgeeks.org/eA8ZMEKiDO

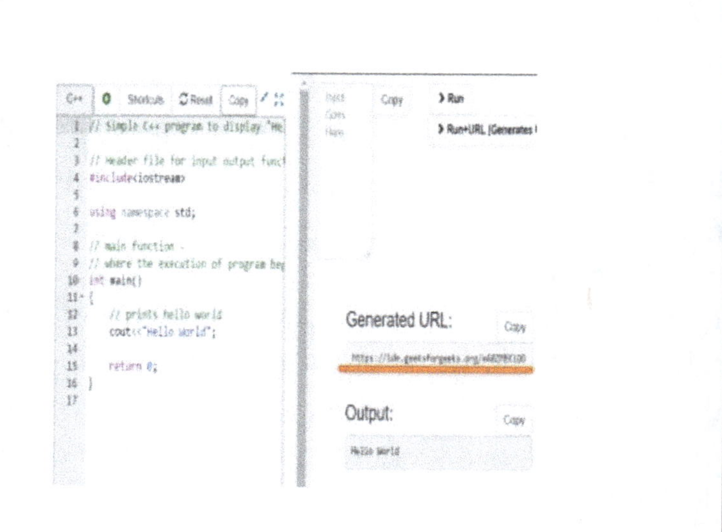

"Hello World" program in GeeksforGeeks IDE

This screenshot is the successful run of "Hello World" in split-screen mode. As we begin to use the IDE for coding exercises, note theinput and output boxes. While there are no inputs for this program,you will input data into the top box labeled "Input Goes Here…"
when prompted by the program in the output below.

You can accessthis program in the saved IDE here:
https://ide.geeksforgeeks.org/eA8ZMEKiDO.

You can also view a copy of the code in the index.

Using Cout

The **cout** object uses the << operator to print values and text, and we can have as many of them as we like. Using the IDE in your browser, change the code to print out:

Hello World

I am learning C++

Like this:

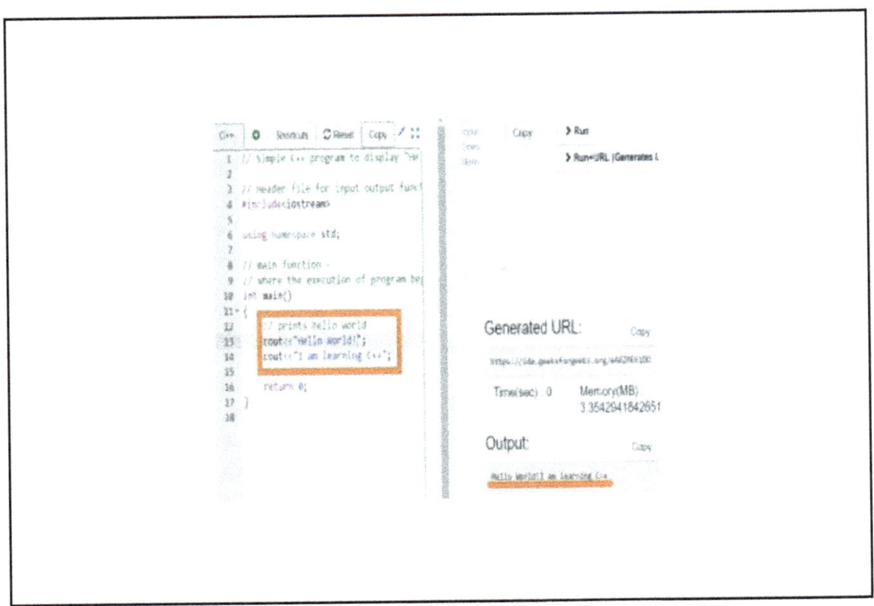

Adding cout objects

This screenshot is the successful run of our edited "Hello World" program in split-screen mode. While the program ran without any errors, it didn't produce the result we wanted. Observing the output, the printed text is missing a new line. We will have to instruct the compiler to add the new line to get the desired result.

Adding lines can be done in several ways: we can add delimiters within the strings or use another manipulator object from the *iostream* library.

Using Escape Sequences

Although it might be tempting to write a string within cout and enter a line, it will not work. It will break the code and it will not run. Don't believe me? Test it!

You can add a new line by using an escape sequence. **Escape sequences** are used in many instances where you need to introduce special characters within strings and character streams. It can alsoadd lines, like so:

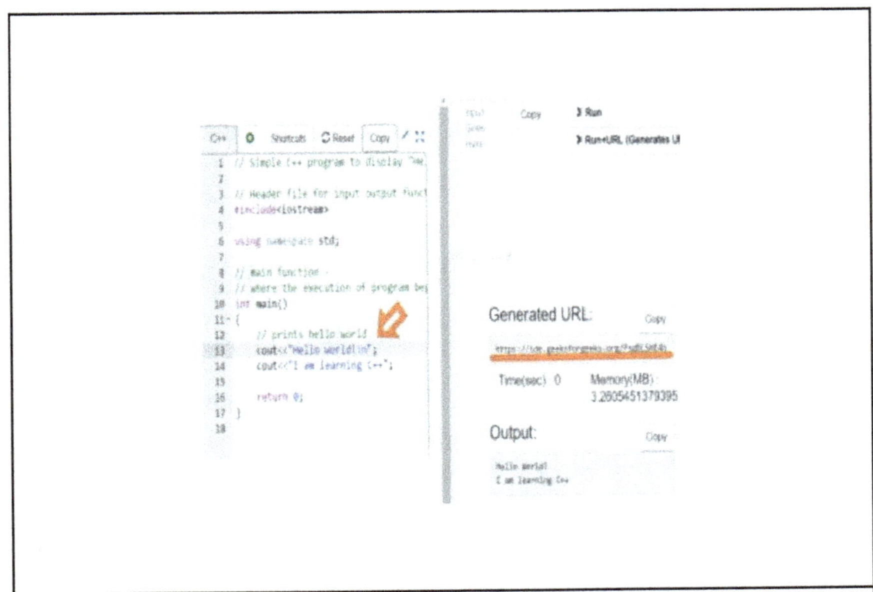

Using in-string escape sequences to delimit and manipulate theoutput

This screenshot is the successful run of our edited "Hello World"

program in split-screen mode. Using $\backslash$n, we were able to get ourexpected output.

As you look at the code, you can see that doubles quotes are used.So, if you want to add double quotes in a string, you will have to use an escape sequence so that the compiler knows that is not a part ofthe code. Not doing so may cause unforeseen errors or bugs. This is why escape sequences matter. Here is a list of the many instances where they can be used ("Escape sequences—Cppreference.com," n.d.):

" \' ": Used for single quotes" \" ": Used for double quotes " \? ": Used for question marks" \\ ": Used for backslashes

"\f": Stands for "form feed" and is used to go to the next "page" "\n": Stands for "line feed" and is used to go to the next line "\t": Stands for "horizonatal tab" and adds 5 spaces horizontally

"\v": Stands for "veritical tab" and is used for spacing in vertical

languages

Note: If you decide to try Escape sequences As different delimiters, be sure to only use the text the

Run button. This will save the workspace.

If you want to save some of your results for later, you

button can use the Run + URL format and the URL... to return to later. To return to our exercise, you can use our saved IDE workspace URL
(https://ide.geeksforgeeks.org/PsgBLSHE4h).

You can also access this code in the index.

Using Endl: Input/Output Manipulators

Like we have said, programming languages are as versatile as human language. You can express one instruction in many ways, and terminating a string is no exception. The difference between an escape sequence and *endl* is that *endl* flushes and refreshes the buffer used to store the string. Programmers use *endl* to clear memory after printing a lot of text. You can see why this is useful in memory management. *Endl* is an example of an input/output manipulator. **Input/Output manipulators** are functions that allow youto control input/output streams using the "<<" operator or the ">>" operator ("Input/output manipulators—Cppreference.com," n.d.).

Like escape sequences, there are many more input/outputmanipulators that give programmers more control over data types or strings. Many of them will make sense once we talk about data types and structuring classes. Here are some of them ("Input/output manipulators—Cppreference.com," n.d.):

": Switches between using "0/1" to"false/true" for Boolean values

boolalpha/noboolapha

showbase/noshowbase

For mathematical outputs, controls whether a

prefix is used to indicate a numeric base

"showpos/noshowpos": Controls whether the " + " sign is used to indicate non-negative numbers

"uppercase/nouppercase": Controls the usage of uppercase characters with particular output formats

"ends": Outputs "\0"

"flush": Flushes the output stream "endl": Outputs "\n" and flushes the output stream "get_money": Receives an input as a monetary value

"put_money": Formats and outputs a monetary value

"get_time": Receives an input as a date/time value according to a specified format

"put_time": Receives an input as a date/time value according to a specified format

Note: Recall our conversation about C++11 and C++14. As of this writing, most programming IDEs use C++11 as their default version. The "get/put…" functions are all in C++11. If you receive an errortrying to use these manipulators, check to see if your setup is using C++11.

Additionally, "**quoted**" is a manipulator that is in C++14 only. This

manipulator allows you to insert and extract quoted strings with embedded spaces ("Input/output manipulators—Cppreference.com," n.d.).

Omitting Namespace

We have already spoken about using *namespace* statements. Wesaid it helps declare strings globally, but when it comes to a small program like "Hello World" it is not so important. For larger programs that use several functions, it is good practice to use the statement to declare each string separately. This saves memory space in the compiler, or you will find yourself in a situation where the compiler is bogged down unnecessarily, having to pull the entire string namespace library to print code. Declaring each string separately might make your code wordier, but it will reduce compiler overhead,and it focuses your instructions. *Std namespace* has multiple objects and definitions that can make it difficult for the computer to find the appropriate way to manipulate and define a string. The namespace convention is important when you have functions that are going to be called by multiple programs. So putting it in there unnecessarily hasthe potential of making your functions poorly defined and causing recognition errors between them.

Let's make our code more efficient by removing the using *namespace*

from our code.

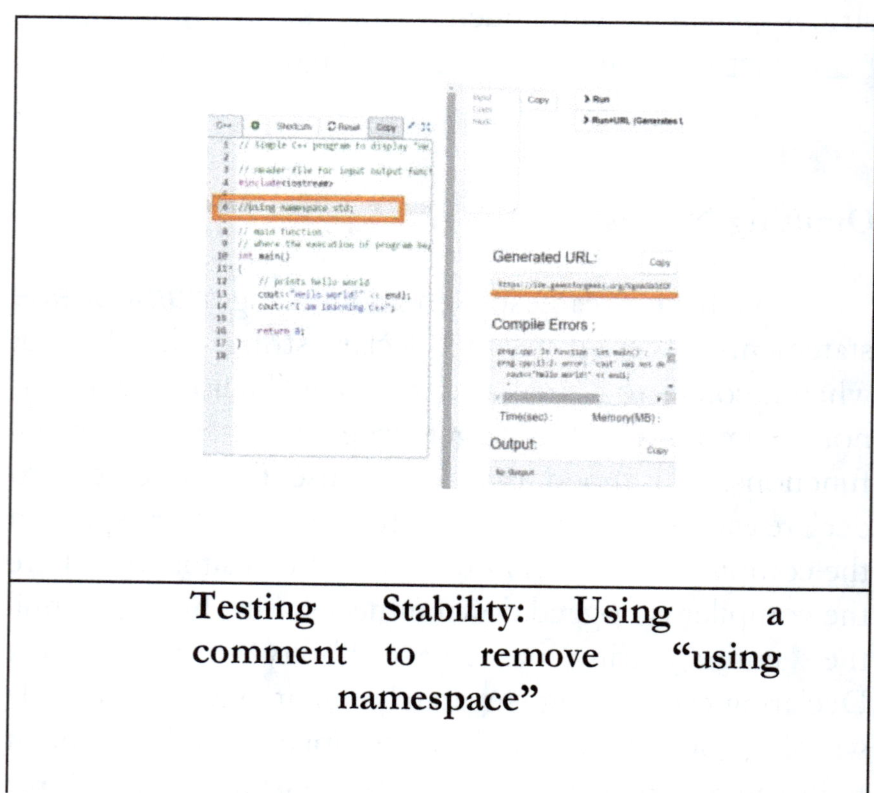

Testing Stability: Using a comment to remove "using namespace"

This screenshot is an unsuccessful test run of the "Hello World" program with **usingnamespacestd;** removed. You can access this saved IDE space through the following URL: https://ide.geeksforgeeks.org/VgobOAOdiX.

"Commenting out" lines of code is a highly efficient way of testingthe stability of code. You can delete the double forward slashes to remove the comment and restore the line of code at any time. This allows you to test the code without destroying it. Once you have completed testing, it is good practice to delete any unwanted lines of code. During your testing, you can always return to this saved instance by using the URL above. You can also access the rawcode in the index.

When you remove *using namespace* std the following error occurs:

```
prog.cpp: In function 'int main()':

prog.cpp:13:2: error: 'cout' was not declared in this
scopecout<<"Hello World!" << endl;

  ^


prog.cpp:13:2: note: suggested alternative:In file
included from prog.cpp:4:0:

/usr/include/c++/5/iostream:61:18:            note:
'std::cout' extern ostream cout; /// Linked to
standard output

  ^


prog.cpp:13:26: error: 'endl' was not declared in
this scopecout<<"Hello World!" << endl;

  ^


prog.cpp:13:26: note: suggested alternative:

In            file            included          from
/usr/include/c++/5/iostream:39:0,from prog.cpp:4:

/usr/include/c++/5/ostream:590:5:            note:
'std::endl'
ndl(basic_ostream<_CharT, _Traits>&____os)

  ^
```

Looking closely, the compiler tells us that we

need to declare *cout*and *endl*. It even makes suggestions, like declaring them as *std*. Let's do as the compiler asks and see what happens.

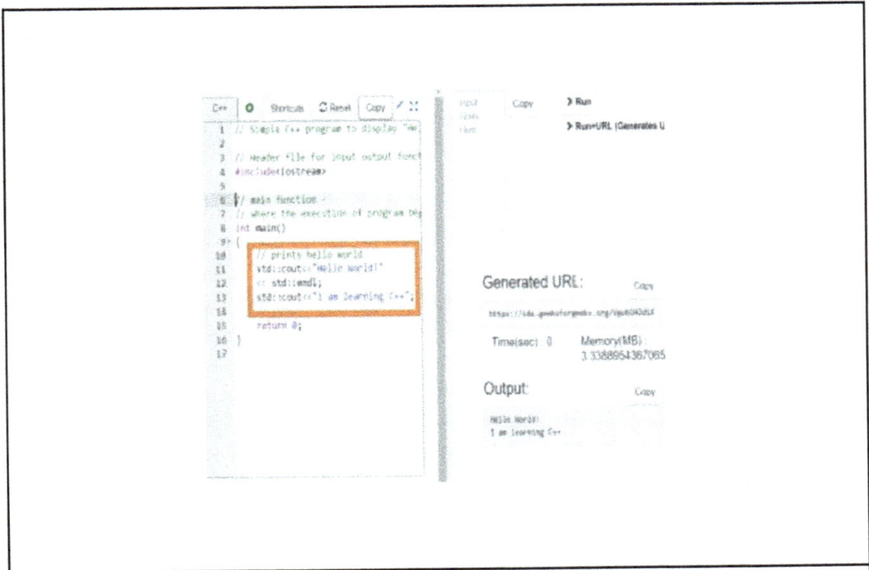

Declaring the iostream objects and manipulators

This screenshot is a successful test run of the "Hello   World"   program   with **usingnamespacestd;** removed.   Once   the iostream objects and manipulators were successfully declared, the unneeded line was removed.

If you would like to practice, you can use this URL: https://ide.geeksforgeeks.org/VgobOAOdiX

Note: If you are having multiple errors during your practice, we will always provide a saved IDE workspace with a successful run of the program to help you troubleshoot. To begin the troubleshooting session, open up another window, and navigate to the successful run. Compare your current workspace with the successful run workspace. You can find a successful run of "Declaring the iostream objects and manipulators"   at   this link:https://ide.geeksforgeeks.org/a5zOdSWoQU.

CHAPTER 3:

VARIABLES AND DATA TYPES

We have talked about how low-level programming is similar to machine language, but they are different because they still use things like syntax, structures, and variables that are similar to human languages. Variables are a mathematical concept that humans use to tell machines what they mean. Speech is made up of a lot of mathematical ideas, which is a big part of computer science. All of these are called AND and OR gates, and they let machines make decisions on a single data bit at a time. People who do a lot of computing work use bitwise functions at a very small level. They can help with everything from controlling displays to switching traffic on a server. Later in Chapter 4, we'll talk about these more advanced topics. For now, let's learn more about C++

by looking at variables.

There are many important things about any programming language, but variables are one of the most important. Functions and other operations in a programming language work on variables. Some programs don't need input or output, but all programs have some variable that they are working on or there's nothing to work on, so that's what we said. The result of a function is always a change in the state it is in at the end. There is a state change when a machine moves from one decision or operational phase to the next one. In old mainframe computers, this term was used to talk about how things worked. It's still used in computer science to talk about how programs work, though. In our example, the IDE started with the main() state already set up before the program started. Then, it changed states so that it could run the output command.

Because lower-level languages are so close to machine language, state changes are talked about a lot because they are so important. They are also called compiled languages because they are turned into machine language when they are written down at a low level. High-level languages like Python don't have to be written in this way. When we talked about how higher-level languages don't need variables to be named with their data types because they have built-in libraries, you might remember that we said that. You can see this in Python, for example. The Python environment lets it know about variables and their data types. C++ has to be written in a way that makes it clear what things are and how they work. There are different types of data. A data type tells the compiler how to deal with it. Vectors in math help us understand data types better. Instead of integers, which show us how much something costs, vectors show us how
60

big or small a space is. Because vectors are different from integers, they are not the same thing. Properties like these are used in programs like Photoshop to help with how things look when they're being drawn.

Note: Vector-based images can be manipulated without losing the quality of the image. This is because files like .jpeg or .png storepixel location of an image as integers on a grid. Vector files such as svg or .pdf use vectors to describe their pixel locations. Therefore, when the image is made larger, the vectors indicate how the colors should expand while the regular image files do not. This is what causes the pixelation and distortion when manipulating non-vector image files.

Input and Output: Declaring Variables

In the previous chapter, we declared some things as we were learning how to use *cout*. In this section, we are going to look at examples of data types and how they are declared. Below are examples of variable declarations and what they stand for ("C++ Variables," n.d.). Keep in mind that variables essentially store types of data:

"int". Keyword is short for "integer" and stores whole numbers, without decimals. This keyword includes positive and negative integers.

"double". Stores numbers with decimals, both positive andnegative numbers.

61

"**char**": Keyword is short for "character" and stores single charactersregardless of their capitalization. Char values are single quoted.

"**string**": Stores text, such as in our "Hello World" example. String values are double quoted.

"**bool**": Keyword is short for "Boolean" and stores values with two states: true or false. As previously discussed, these values can be expressed as either "0/1" or "false/true."

In the next section, we will discuss them in detail. Now let us look at examples of these. To create a variable you have to assign it a valueafter the "=" operator. Their syntax looks like this:

[Datatype][Variable_name] = [value];

Note: Each **[Variable_name]** must be unique within your function. Otherwise, it will cause an error.

Now let us create a variable called "*myNum*" with the *int* data type and a value of 10, then have our program print it out.

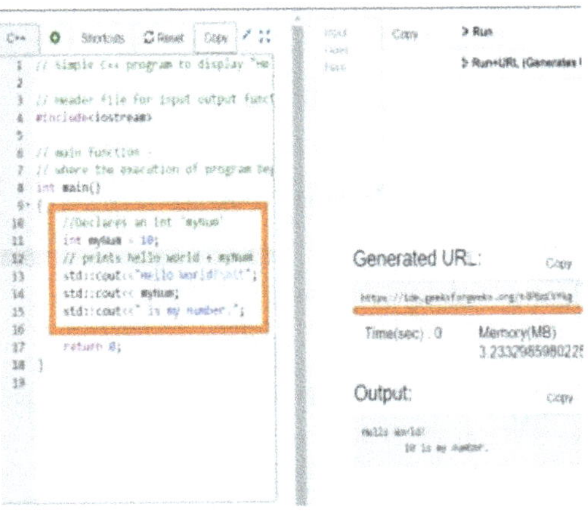

Declaring int numbers

This screenshot is a successful test run of the "myNum" program. You can access the saved IDE workspace with the following URL: https://ide.geeksforgeeks.org/t4P6qCVfkg.

This code was implemented without **usingnamespacestd;** as it's the best practice. You should practice implementing the same code successfully with the namespace. Remember that you can reset the workspace to a successful state by using the URL.

We had our share of *cout* examples in our code. Let's use the input box in the top right and the *cin* object so our program takes in inputs and operates on them.

We can do this by writing programs that take two numbers and adds them together. To do this, we have to declare two variables that will store our inputs for our program to operate on.

We will declare multiple variables:

Two *int* variables named *x* and *y*,

One *int* variable named sum.

We can also tell the program to prompt the user to give two inputs.

Note: In our IDE, you must enter the inputs *before* you run the program. Each input should be on its own line.

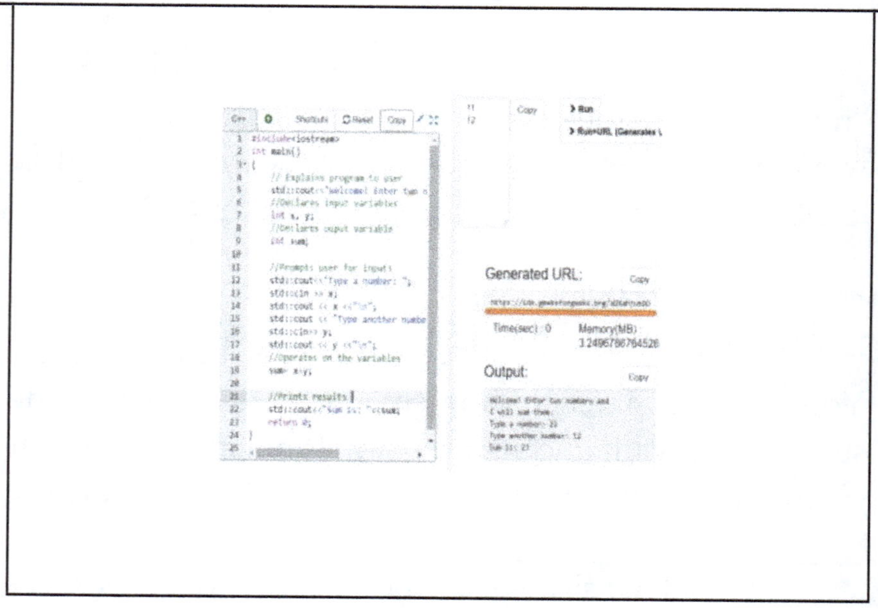

Summing inputs and printing the result

This screenshot is a successful test run of our "Summing" program. You can access the saved IDE workspace with the following URL: https://ide.geeksforgeeks.org/xDXaHjutDO. This exercise had to be modified for our IDE's input system. Therefore, we included

additional lines that confirm our inputs.

This code was implemented without **usingnamespacestd;** as it's the best practice. You should practice implementing the same codesuccessfully with the namespace. Remember that you can reset the workspace to the successful state by using the URL.

cout

Basic Data Types

Data types specify the size and types of information stored in a variable. Each has its own keyword and an associated size ("C++ Data Types," n.d) :

" **int**": Keyword is short for "integer" and stores whole numbers. Has a size of 4 bytes.

" **float**": Stores decimal numbers with 7 decimal digits. Has a size of 4 bytes.

" **double**": Stores decimals numbers with 15 decimal digits. Has a sizeof 8 bytes.

" **char**": Keyword is short for "character" and stores single characters regardless of their capitalization. Has a size of 1 byte.

" **bool**": Keyword is short for "boolean" and stores values that have a state of either being true or false. Has a size of 1 byte.

Note: Recall the "**string**" data type. We have worked with this specialdatatype extensively. String values can vary in size. Due to this, they are handled in the iostream library to apply more flexibility for text handling. We'll return to strings and discuss some advanced topics in the next section.

These sizes matter for data handling. For instance,

when you use *int* with *float/double* all those numbers will be converted to *int*. It is because the compiler uses 4 bytes to calculate integers which havethe allocation for decimals. The program will still run but your calculations will not be accurate. Let's explore this more by modifying our program and looking at the results. We are going to be using a long-popular decimal number (pi):

$$\frac{22}{7} = 3.14285714$$

It will test the limits of float and double.

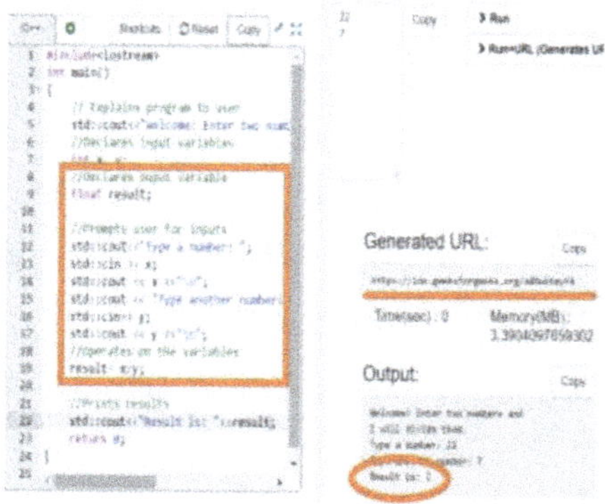

Using Int with Float or Double

This screenshot is a successful test run of our modified prog
calculating

$= \frac{22}{7}$. You can access the saved IDE workspace with the following URL:
https://ide.geeksforgeeks.org/a8Mw6tmyf8
. This exercise also includes $\frac{22}{7}$

$= 3.142857142857142857142857142857$

...

but as you can see, the result is shown as 3. This is because the compiler calculated the inp
int

, which are not modified to store decimals. As a result, the
missing the decimals.

To get the result we are looking for, it would be best to change the variable data types. Will using float data types differ from double data types? Can we expect a different result? Remember you can reset by going to a successful state of the workspace using the URL.

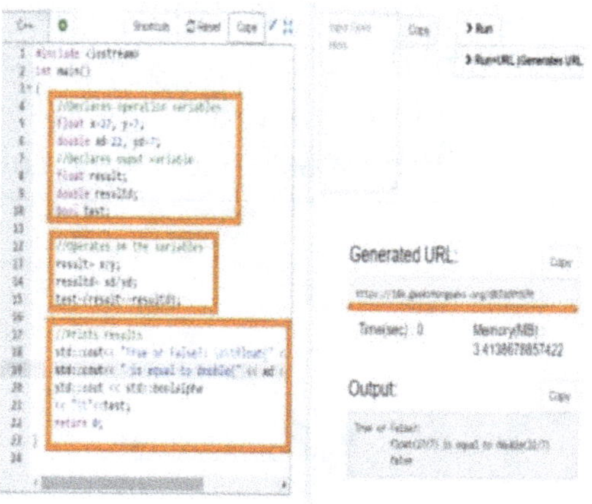

Π

$= \frac{22}{7}$. To focus on comparing float and doubl

 bool

boolalpha/noboolapha

Comparing Float and Double

This screenshot is a successful test run of our modified program calculating

We have removed the input statements and rearranged our data types. We highly suggest creating this program for yourself using the previous   program located   at   this   URL: https://ide.geeksforgeeks.org/a8Mw6tmyf8.   This exercise will give you practice in some previous coding topics we discussed, including:

"   " data type keyword

"   " input-output manipulator

It will also give you some experience with a logical operator. We will discuss the logical operators in detail in the next chapter. Once you have manipulated the program, open a new window, and compare this to the successful run of the screenshot above. You can find the saved IDE workspace with the successful run at this URL: https://ide.geeksforgeeks.org/dNIUdYtN7M.

Power of C++: Advanced Strings

Another data type we are going to look at is strings. **Strings** are one of the most popular data types in computer science; they are sequences of characters. It might be helpful to think of them as sentences, but not every sentence represents a string. We haveseen how they work with our "Hello World" app. Strings are a separate data type with their own library. To manipulate and work with them a program needs an appropriate header – the string library. These libraries have methods and features that allow the program to manipulate strings.

Operation: String Concatenation

String concatenation is when different strings are put together into one string. It is combining strings. This is one of the most common functions of a program. For instance, when you enter your name at awebsite or a game and then you switch to another page and the screen greets you "Hello, [your_name]!", the program has used concatenation to do that. It has combined "Hello," with your name and "!" in the end.

In C++, string concatenations are performed through the "+" operator. Let's see this in action by making a program that prints an imputed string with a greeting. For this to work, we must include the

<string> library, which contains objects and statements needed for handling strings.

Open a fresh instance of the IDE we have been using and follow these steps:

In addition to

#include

< iostream > , also include the string >

library

Omit usingnamespacestd;

Remove the current filler code within intmain(){...}

Declare and set the variables

firstName = "John" and lastName = Doe

Declare and calculate

fullName by adding firstName and lastName with the " +

" operator

Print out the result as "Hello John Doe." It should look something like this:

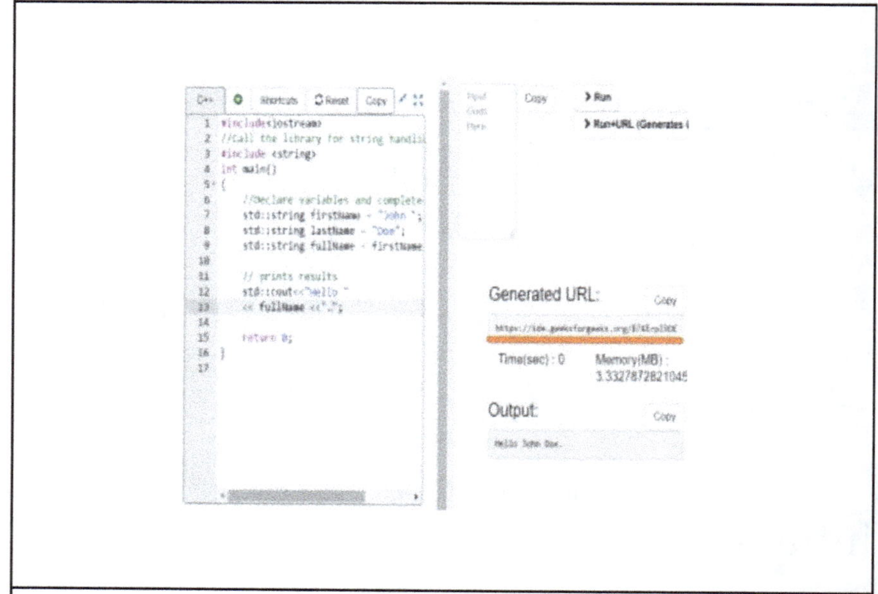

String Concatenation

This screenshot is a successful test run of our string concatenation program. We encourage you to open up this program in another window and compare it to your program. You can access the successful run at this URL: https://ide.geeksforgeeks.org/B7XErpI9OE.

Note: Be sure to annotate your code. You can shorthand the instructions and use them as an impromptu algorithm to annotate your code. This will help you keep the program in order.

Usually, in forums, the concatenated text input is kept small as possible and the formatting is done by the program. In the example, we manually have to add space after "Hello" and "John", but the program adds space. Now that you have seen how the "+" operator works, how might you add space? See if you can figure it out by playing with the code in your editor. If things fall apart you canalways return to our successful IDE workspace by clicking on the URL.

Note:

The "+" operator is used for both adding numbers and concatenatingstrings.Trying to use the operator to add a string and a number will produce an error.You can test this on your own using a modified program from the previous chapter.You can also check out a successful run of the program here that shows how to concatenate numbers as strings at this URL:

https://ide.geeksforgeeks.org/glPmslDwF7.Uncom ment thedeclarations to try to add numbers and strings to see the error for yourself.The error is very long and verbose,as it conflicts across the

<*iostream*> and <*string*>libraries.

String Objects: Length() Attribute

We know from real-world experience that strings, like many things, can come in different sizes. This is unlike other data types we have xplored so far. C++ makes this possible because it construes strings as objects with attributes. C++ defines a string length under the *Length*() attribute as you would expect in an object. To access length, the string must be attached to a variable and you must use the "." syntax. It should look something like this:

[*string_name*].*length*()

Let's return to our program and retrieve the length of *fullName*. We will need to modify our code by adding a new line with the syntax above and another *cout*, like this:

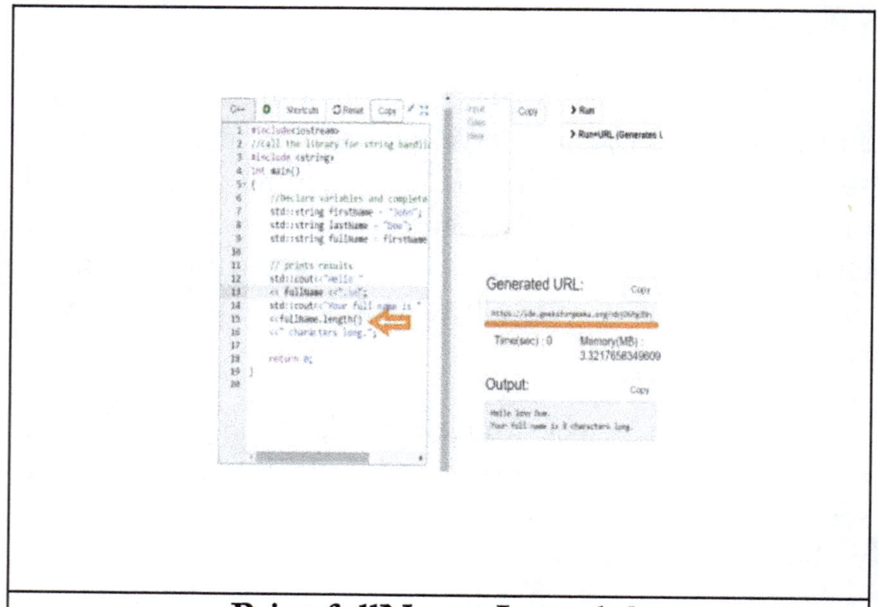

Print fullName.Length()

This screenshot is a successful test run of our modified stringconcatenation program. We encourage you to modify the program at this URL: https://ide.geeksforgeeks.org/B7XErpI9OE.

Once you have modified the program, you can compare it to this successful test run by opening it in another window. You can access this saved IDE window at the following URL: https://ide.geeksforgeeks.org/xbjO6Pg3Nh.

String Indexes and Arrays

Recall our conversation on objects. Vector arrays are also a special mathematical phenomenon with their own special attributes. An **array** is an orderly arrangement of objects – often rows, columns, or a matrix – where each has its own specific location. Strings are stored in arrays made up of characters. Therefore, a string array is orderly arrangements of characters where each character in a string is indexed in its own location. Arrays are accessed by using [ ] to finda character or any other items in an array. String indexes start with [0]. Let's see this in action by changing our program so that it prints out the 3rd character in *fullName*.

Note:

Remember that the index starts with [0].Therefore the 3rd character in the string array would be at [2], not 3.

We are going to use this syntax to do so:

fullName[*x*]

The *x* stands for the index of the character we would like to print out.Remember to also edit the cout to properly print the letter. You will also need to use escape sequences like this:

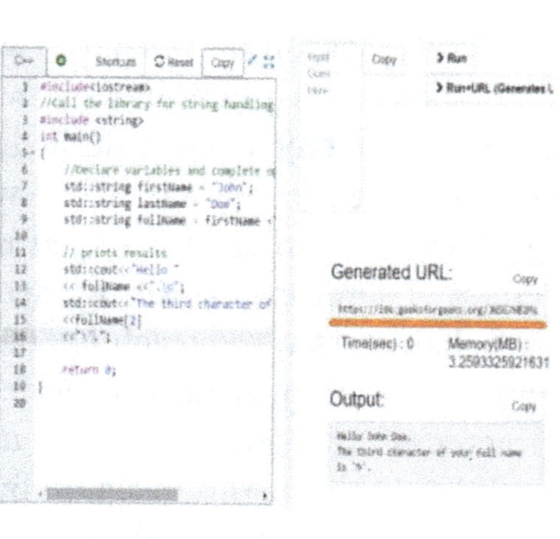

Access fullName String Array

This screenshot is a successful test run of our modified stringattributes program. We encourage you to modify the program atthis URL:

https://ide.geeksforgeeks.org/xbjO6Pg3Nh.

Once you have modified the program, you can compare it to this successful test run by opening it in another window. You can access this saved IDE window at the following URL: https://ide.geeksforgeeks.org/JWSG7HB2Ms.

In our examples we have relied a lot on *cout* capabilities, but, as I have alluded to, there are other strings handling capabilities used by programmers to field content from different sources. These are *cin* objects and the *getline*() function.

Cin and getline() function

In examples from the previous chapter, we have used *cin*. Like **cout**, **cin** is an object in the *<iostream>* library and it allows a program to receive input using the ">>" operator. Like **cout**, **cin** objects must be defined with the std data type. Let's modify our concatenation programs so that it receives the input of "John Doe". You can use your name if you like, as it can be fun to do so. You will need tofollow these instructions:

Navigate to the string concatenator program at the followingURL:

https://ide.geeksforgeeks.org/B7XErpI9OE

Declare the variables

Prompt the user for their name

Calculate the operation by using the following

....fullName
          = firstName + "" + lastName...
code snippet:

Print the results

If you find yourself stuck, here is how it should look:

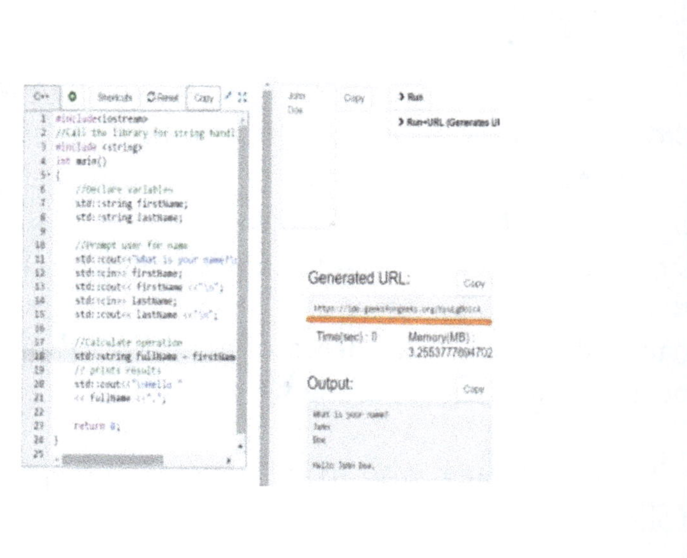

String Concatenation with cin

This screenshot is a successful test run of our modified string

concatenation program using **cin**. We encourage you to open up this program in another window and compare it to your program. You can access the successful run at this URL: https://ide.geeksforgeeks.org/KyuLgBoicA.

Note: Be sure to annotate your code. You can shorthand the instructions and use them as an impromptu algorithm to annotate your code. This will help you keep the program in order.

The program will work only when the user enters their first and last name separately. But most peoples 'names are stored or put in as one single string. Let's change our program so that it greets the user when they enter their full name. You will need to follow these steps:

If not there already, or you need to reset the workspace, go to theprevious workspace at the following URL:

https://ide.geeksforgeeks.org/KyuLgBoicA

Declare only the variable **fullName**

Prompt the user for their full name using **cin**

Greet the user using **cout and the input fullName**

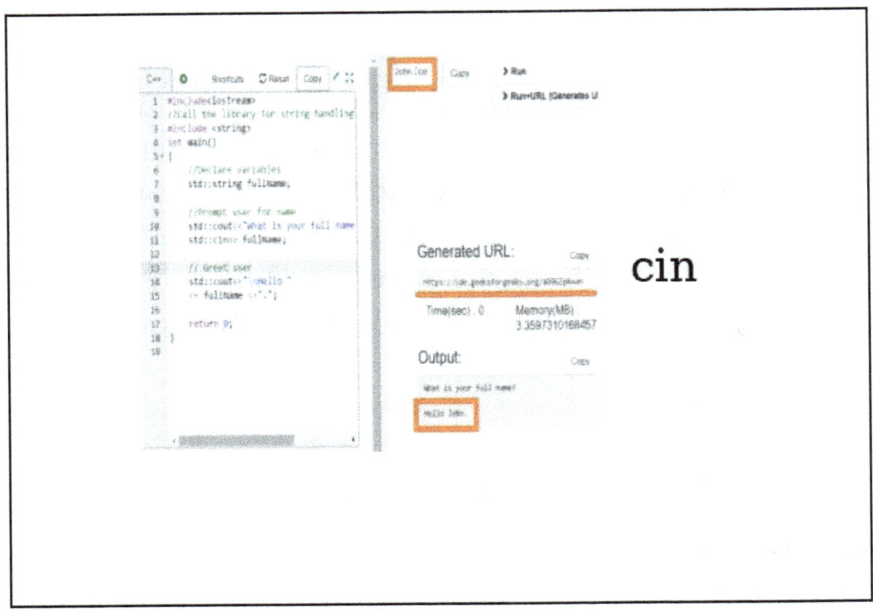

You have witnessed typical *cin* behavior. When *cin* encounters a space it reads it as a string terminator and stops. This is why "Doe"is not added to the output. To get it to read the entire string with spaces, we must use the *getline*() function from the <string> library;it extracts all characters from the input and turns them into a string array.

Note:

getline()is usually preferred over *cin* to ensure that programs can read fielded text from secondary sources,particularly since *getline*() can read and aggregate different sorts of characters without errors.

Here is an example of *getline*() functions used well: https://www.geeksforgeeks.org/getline-string-c/

In this chapter, we have done quite a bit. We have looked at specialized functions, accessing objects, text manipulators, and operators. We will cover them in more detail in the coming chapters.I hope you have seen the role of operators in directing data and lending program functionality. In the following chapter, we are going to be looking at operators and how they give programs decision-making capabilities.

CHAPTER 4:

OPERATIONS IN C++

We talked about how C++ is mostly a back-end, server-side language that can be used to control servers and other tools for delivering content. Finally, we looked at how C++ deals with data by looking at strings. There, we saw that operations play a very important role in the world around us. Operations let us control the loops and decisions in programs, so we can make sure they work the way they

84

should. We can add more functionality to our programs if we know more about how things work. Functionality is how programmers use the tools and methods of a language to reach their goal. They work, but it would be better to use these features in a way that allows us to reach our goal, like content management, instead.

Note: "Operand" describes the value or variable being operated on. "Operator" describes the symbol indicating the sort of operation being carried out ("C++ Operators," n.d.).

The following is a list of operators in C++ ("Operators-In-C.png (800×533)," n.d.):

Operator	Type
$++, --$	Unary operator > Arithmetic
$+, -, *, /, \%$	Binary operator > Arithmetic
$<, <=, >, >=, ==, !=$	Binary operator > Relational
$, \|\|, !$	Binary operator > Logical
$, \|, <<, >>, \sim, \wedge$	Binary operator > Bitwise
$=, +=, -=, *=, /=, \% =$	Binary operator > Assignment
$?:$	Ternary or conditional operator

This table lists the operator symbols and categorizes them by (1)how many operands they accept at a time > (2) the type of operation they implement. For example, most arithmetic operators operate on two operands at a time.

All operators are characterized by how many operands they can operate on at a time and the types of operations they can execute. They are divided into three types:

Unary - operators that only accept 1 operand at a time

Binary - operators that only accept 2 operands at a time

Ternary - operators that accept more than 2 operands, or conditionaloperators with several arguments

They are further divided into 6 more types:

Arithmetic

Relational

Logical

Bitwise

Assignment operators

Other operators such as a conditional, address, andredirection

In this chapter, we will look at 5 types of operators and their functionalities.

Note: Operators have precedence, just as in mathematical equations. For example, parentheses, which are used to call a function, have higher precedence than addition or subtraction. However, you should try to keep your lines of code as simple as possible. This makes your programs easier to edit and debug. Having clean, uncomplicated code avoids bugs.

Binary Operators

Binary operators are the majority of operands you find in C++. They include 5 of the 6 types of operators. This makes them the perfectplace to start. As the name suggests, binary operators compare two operands. They are perfect for decision-making and controlling switches.

Arithmetic Operators

They are the most common and well understood of all operators because of how much we use them even outside programming, since they are primarily mathematical. We use them to perform mathematical operations.

Note: In the string concatenation example, the " " used to concatenate *was not an arithmetic function*. Instead, it was a functionof the **< string >** library that handled the concatenation.

Most operators in this category require two operands. The only exceptions are the unary "++" and " --" operators which we use to increase or decrease within a loop. The binary operators are (Jaggi, 2015a):

"**+**": the addition operator that adds two operands

"**–**": the subtraction operator that subtracts one operand from another "*****": the multiplication operator that multiplies two operands

"**/**": the division "forward slash" operator that divides the first operand into the second

"**%**": the modulus operator that returns the remainder from dividing the first operand into the second

Let's make a *cout* program that demonstrates all of these 5 arithmetic operands. Create a new C++ workspace in the IDE and follow these instructions:

Declare two variables **a** integers **a = 25** and b = 3

Declare a variable, **result**

Print the variables **a and b**

Add **a and b** and print the result

Subtract **a and b** and print the result

Multiply **a and b** and print the result

Divide **a and b** and print the result

Calculate the remainder from dividing and print the resultHere is how that looks.

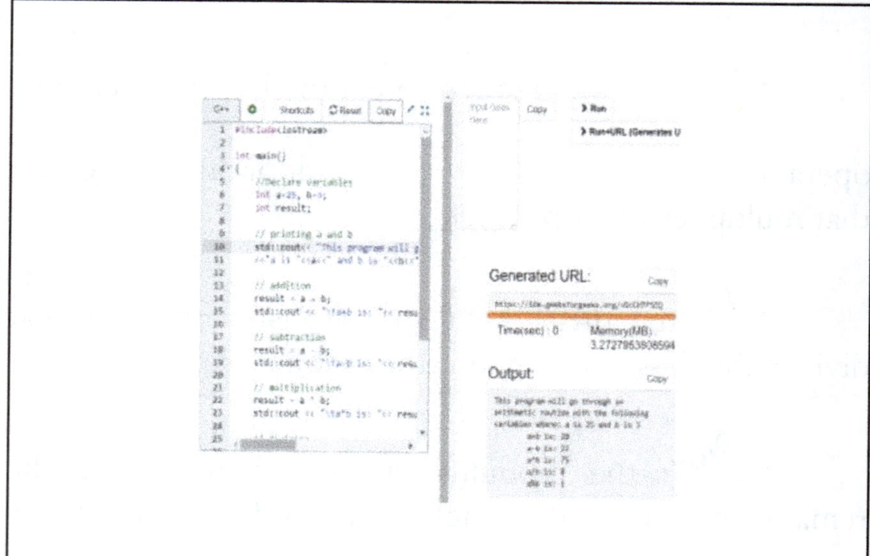

Arithmetic Routine Program

This screenshot is a successful run of the arithmetic routine program displaying all the arithmetic functions. You can access a copy of the raw code in the index.

If you get errors, I encourage you to use our successful run to troubleshoot your workspace. Open it up to compare the code. Here is where to find it:

https://ide.geeksforgeeks.org/vDcCH7f5EQ

Relational Operators

Most programs, not just in C++, use conditionals and loops to control flow. Operators in this section are used to perform conditional switching. For instance, in games, the game engine adapts to how the player interacts with the game. It gives the gamer more of an engaging and dynamic experience.

If the gamer completes challenges quickly, it might mean they find the game too easy. As a result, the game adjusts by increasing difficulty, but not too much. If the game is too hard, the engine might respond to that by making it a little easier to play. This is called dynamic gameplay,and it happens because coding languages have conditional switching. Conditional switching, the adaptation, happens through relational operators that compare two values. All relational operators are binary (Jaggi, 2015b). Here they are:

" **==** ": "Equal" operator that checks whether two given operands areequal. If the operands are equal, it returns a Boolean "true"; if not, it returns false.

" **!=** ": "Not-Equal" operator that also checks whether two given operands are equal or not. However, this operator returns a Boolean true if the operands are not equal and returns false if the operands are equal.

" **>** ": "Greater-than" operator that checks if the operand on the left is greater than the operand on the right. If so, this operator returns a Boolean true. Otherwise, it returns false.

"   <   ": "Less-than" operator that checks if the operand on the left is less than the operand on the right. If so, this operator returns a Boolean true. It returns Boolean false otherwise.

"   >=   ": "Greater-than or equal-to" operator that checks if the operandon the left is greater than or equal to the operand on the right. If so,this operand returns a Boolean true. If not, it returns a Boolean false.

<=   ": "Lesser-than or equal-to" operator that checks whether the operand on the left is less than or equal to the operand on the right. If so, this operand returns a Boolean true. If not, it returns false.

Like we did with the arithmetic operators, let's create a **cout** program which demonstrates relational operators, We are going to be using conditional **if()** statements in our code. An **if()** statement executes the code within its curly braces when a specified condition is met. If the condition is not met it will execute the code in the **else**{} statement. Theelse does not have a condition to check; it executes when the specifiedcondition in **if()** is not met. Conditional statements always use a relational operator to test a condition.

Note:

The **if()**) and else statement is case sensitive.Both "if" and "else" must be lowercase.Additionally,while if()

can be executed without an else,the missing else statement can cause an error if the condition is false.else statements also cannot be implemented without an if()statement.We will describe if()...else statements in more detail in later chapters

To create our program we have to follow the following steps.

Open and edit the arithmetic routine program using this URL:

https://ide.geeksforgeeks.org/vDcCH7f5EQ

Use the same variables from the arithmetic routine. Be sure to clean the code of any unneeded variables.

Print an explanation of the program

Test $if(a > b)$ and print the result

Create an if statement printing out the result if greater than

Create a nested else statement printing out the result if false

Note:

if()...else you will have to create a cout

For each for all possibilities. For our simple program, it is only two possibilities for eachstatement.

Test $if(a >= b)$ and print the result

Test $if(a < b)$ and print the result

Test $if(a <= b)$ and print the result

Test $if(a == b)$ and print the result

Test $if(a! = b)$ and print the result

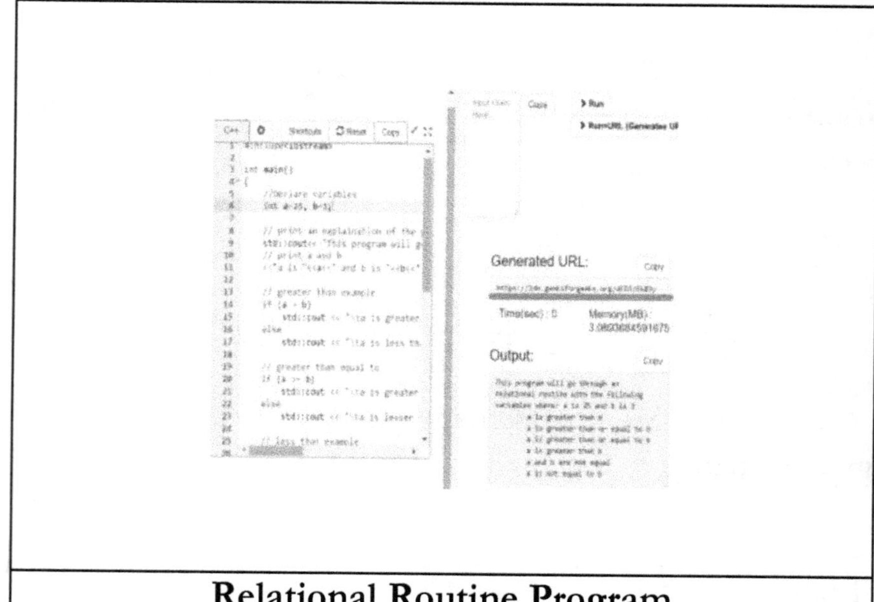

Relational Routine Program

This screenshot is a successful run of the relational routine programdisplaying all the relational functions.

If you did not get similar results, go look at our code here: https://ide.geeksforgeeks.org/dFD3cEk85y. Compare and figure out where you went wrong. An exercise like this one will equip you with debugging skills.

Also, take your time to appreciate the code and understand it.

Logical Operators

Logical operators add more complexity to relational operators. These are comparable to human ideas of "and" or "or". They also have qualities that switch the meaning of the relational operator. **Logical operators** are used in conjunction with relational operators to combine two or more conditions to describe a constraint. They make us catch a lot more and do a lot more with our conditionals. There are three logical operators (Jaggi, 2015b):

"": the logical "AND" operator returns a Boolean true when both the conditions are met and false if they aren't.

" ||": the logical "OR" operator returns a Boolean true when one (or both) of the conditions are met, and false if none of the conditions are met.

" ! ": the logical "NOT" operator returns a Boolean true if the conditions in consideration are not satisfied. If one of the conditions is true, then it returns a Boolean false.

Logical operators are used a lot in machines. Imagine a "NOT" operator in the security system of a bank. Let's say locked doors are "0"[false], and unlocked doors are "1". Because the bank should stay secure, our default value is "0." This is called a failed closed system, because if things go wrong the doors will be closed (the default). All signals that go to the door are controlled by a "NOT" signal: If nothingis going on, the doors should remain locked, and if there is robberythey should also remain locked. Doors that open during a robbery will get a "NOT" signal to fail-close. But in a fire, these doors should open, so the fail-closed "NOT" signal will return true to open doors.

Let's explore logical operators by building a logical routine program. Follow these instructions:

Open and edit the relational routine program using this URL:https://ide.geeksforgeeks.org/dFD3cEk85y

Edit these additional variables to test the logical

$$a = 5, b = 0, c = 12, d = 24$$

operators:

Print an explanation of the program

Test if(a>b && c==d) and print the result

Create an if statement printing out the result if greater than

Create a nested else statement printing out the result if false

Test (a>b || c==d) and print the result

Test (!b) and print the result

Clean the code of any unnecessary linesHere is how it looks:

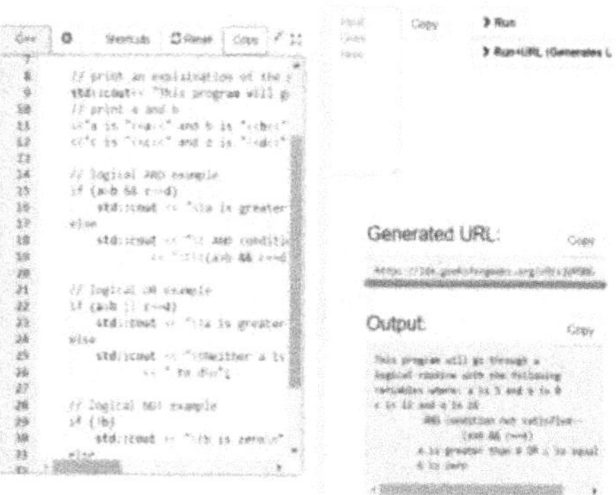

if()...else statement when producing a false
- state. Either relational expression can be false to produce a false AND. However, the program can be fixed to produce an exact answer by r
if()...else

if()...else

Logical Routine Program

This screenshot is a successful run of the logical routine program displaying examples of all the logical functions. You can access this workspace with this URL: https://ide.geeksforgeeks.org/x9ixjUYDBG

As you can see, the "AND" function may be difficult to print with justone

statements. Modify this exercise to create a program that can explainitself better!

Hint: You only need one additional statement. You cancheck your work against ours with this URL -- https://ide.geeksforgeeks.org/nh8yYV9Kjy.

Let's take a break from routines and explore other ways we can use logical operators. Logical operators are based on machine logic, especially logical gates. Logical gates are electronic circuits that have one or more inputs while having one output. Logical gates have the same function as logical operators. "AND" gates only pass "1" when all inputs are "1"; "OR" gates pass "1" when they receive a "1" from any of their inputs; "NOT" passes "1" when they receive a "0" as their input.

Logical gates can control the flow of data in a

circuit, the same as our logical operations when combined with a conditional statement. It is called a **conditional short-circuit** in logical operators.

Logical AND operators and OR operators short-circuit. Recall howlogical AND returns a true Boolean value when both relational operators are conditionally true. What's more, relational operators are assessed in the order that they appear in a conditional statement – if the first one is false the second one will not be evaluated, so it short circuits.

OR operators do this differently. Only one relational operator has to return true for it passes a true Boolean value. So if the first relational operator returns true, it won't check the next one.

This is very useful because we can give more complex instructions to aprogram about how to behave in what circumstances. OR and ANDare short-circuit opposites. Let's use this to write a program that tells when a condition short-circuits AND and OR gates.

Follow these instructions:

Open a new IDE workspace

Declare two   variables:

a = 10,b = 4

Print an explanation of the program

This program will test if the OR gate or the AND gate shorts when ais equal to b.

Print current values of a and b

Declare and calculate two   variables:
bool

resAND = ((a == b) && std::cout << "OR circuit shorted")

resOR = ((a == b) || std::cout << "AND circuit shorted")This is how it looks:

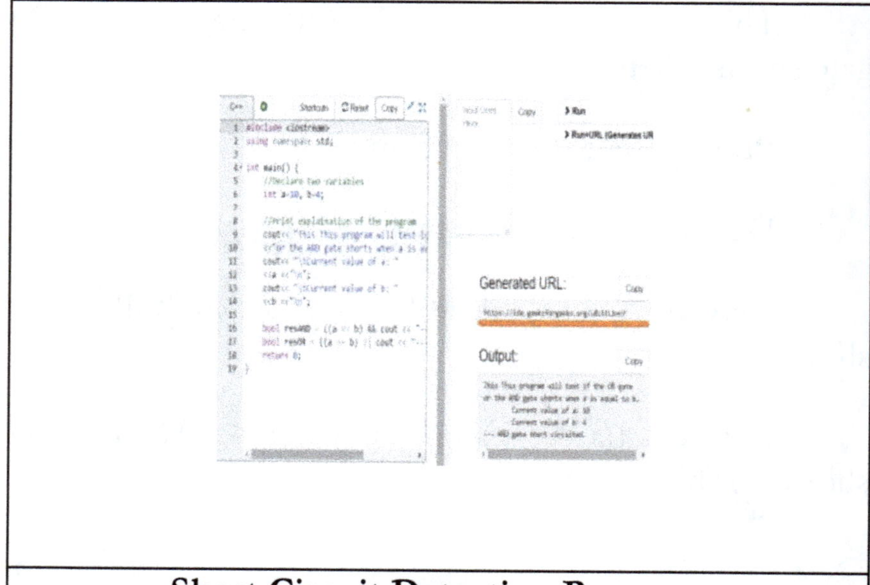

Short Circuit Detection Program

This screenshot is a successful run of our short circuit detectionprogram. Using our knowledge of logical AND, logical OR, and their relationship to each other, we were able to develop a way to detect short circuits. You can access this workspace with this URL: https://ide.geeksforgeeks.org/uBLGtLbnnY

Try different values of a and b to see if you can trip the different"circuits."

Consider a short circuit detection program. How would we use it in the real world? I have alluded to systems like these playing a role in bank security. The question is how it would achieve those things? You can tell your program that if a condition is not ("NOT") met to refuse access, like if the password does not match.

An understanding of logical operators gives a good idea of how machines and systems make their decisions. Relational and logical operators give us more control over what happens in the program and how it relates to everything around it. We do this through variouslibraries, statements, and objects. So far we have written small programs, but in bigger programs using objective control like these cancause overhead for the compiler. That has a noticeable effect in programming environments and industries like gaming engines, content delivery, and others. Think about the servers at YouTube that have to deliver gigabytes of data per second and gaming engines that need to render in real-time: they have to reduce the amount of overhead while being able to utilize these control features. Thankfully, that can be achieved by using bitwise operators.

Bitwise Operators

On the circuit level, machines communicate by using AND and OR gates. It gives them decision-making capabilities at a single bit data level. **Bitwise operators** use those microscopic level calculations to access computing processes at the machine level, bypassing objective programming. In other words, they are logical operators operating on numbers at a binary level.

To use them, you will need to know about binary. Humans conceptualize numbers using **base-10** numbers, also known as the decimal system. For instance, a number like 543 is understood as five-hundreds, three tens, and 4

$$5 * 10^2 + 3 * 10^1 + 4 * 10^0 = 534$$

single units. In base 10 it looks like this:

In binary the same number would look like this 0b1000010110 – the "0b" is just for us humans to understand it is a binary number. Binary numbers are **base-2**, they just look different. All binary numbers are presented as a stream of bits, which can either be in two states: 1 or 0. Like in base-10, the position of the number determines its value. The

534 example shows a binary number that is 10 bits long. Looking closely at the 534 streams we can see that the 2nd, 3rd, 4th, and 10th bits are on (moving right to left), and all the other bits are off (1 is on, 0is off). In base

$$2^9 + 2^4 + 2^2 + 2^1 = 534$$

2 we calculate this as:

It is not easy for us humans to calculate it, but this is how computers communicate, in streams of data bits. They are more adept at recognizing and counting these numbers just as easily as if they were base-10 numbers to humans. Therefore, using bitwise operators that function at the computer's natural level improves speed and performance (Killian, 2012) because it skips the translation of objective programming into machine language. This is why you will find bitwise operations are often used in competitive programming. Below is a listof C++ bitwise operators ("Bitwise Operators in C/C++," 2014):

"": Bitwise AND takes two numbers (operands) and runs AND on every bit within the stream of those numbers. The results of the AND stream will be 1 if both are 1.

"|": Bitwise OR takes two numbers(operands) and runs OR on everybit within the stream of those numbers. The results of the OR stream is 1 if any of the two is 1.

" ∧ " Bitwise XOR that takes two numbers as operands and doesXOR on every bit within the stream of the two numbers. The result stream of XOR is 1 if the two bits are different.

" << " Left shift operator takes two numbers and left shifts the bits ofthe first operand. The second operand is used to determine the number of places to shift.

" >> " Right shift operator takes two numbers and right shifts the bitsof the first operand. The second operand is used to determine the number of places to shift.

" ~ " Bitwise NOT operator that takes one number and switches the state of all the bits (1s to 0s, 0s to 1s).

Note: Machines use registers and buffers to store the bits for calculation. A **register** is just an array of storage, where each bit gets its own place in the array. If

105

you think of these data streams as an array, it will help you rationalize many of the bitwise operators, particularly the shift operators.

Let's write a bitwise routine program. First, we will need to create a bit register and study bit streams. This requires the bitset<x>() function forthe *<bitset>* library. It allows you to print a binary stream with a lengthof <x>. Follow the instructions:

Open a new IDE C++ workspace

In addition to

< iostream > , be sure to call the < bitset >

library as well

Declare the operand variables and their values

unsignedinta = 60;//60 = 0011110

unsignedintb = 13;//13 = 0000110

Declare register c for the calculations

intc = 0;

Print operand values and their registers:

cout << "Operandregistersa:" << a

<< "andb:" << b

```cpp
<< "\n\tregistera: - 0b" << bitset < 8 > (a)

    << "\n\tregisterb: - 0b" << bitset < 8 > (b)
    << endl;
```

Note: Since all numbers are less than 255, we will then use a bitstream of < 8 > for the entire exercise.

Calculate Bitwise AND for

a and b in register c

```cpp
c = ab;//12 = 00001100
```

c

Print the result and the register in

Note: Since we are using bitwise functions, it is better to use `endl;` to terminate our lines. This is because this function clears the buffer and prevents overflow. This makes the program a little slower, but it ensures that our registers are clear. The speed difference is made up by using bitwise functions.

Calculate Bitwise OR for

a and b in register c

```cpp
c = a|b;//61 = 00111101
```

c

Print the resulting value and the register in

Calculate Bitwise XOR for a and b in register

```
c = a^b;//49 = 00110001
```

Print the resulting value and the register in

Calculate Bitwise NOT for a in register c

```
c = ~a;// - 61 = 11000011
```

Print the resulting value and the register in

Print a comparison register for a in register c

This will make it easier to compare with the shifting bitwiseoperations

Calculate Bitwise Left Shift for $a << 2$ in regis

```
c = a << 2;//240 = 11110000
```

Print the result and the register in c

Calculate Bitwise Left Shift for

a >> 2 in register c

$$c = a >> 2;//15 = 00001111$$

Print the result and the register in   C

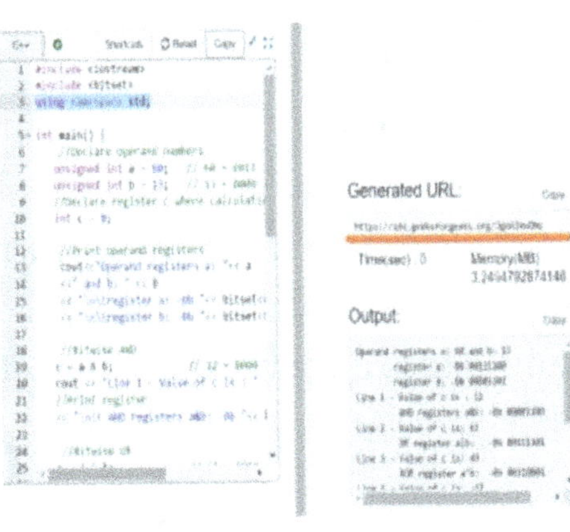

Bitwise Routine with Register Printing

This screenshot is a successful run of our bitwise routine program.

The output features visuals of the   register array. This will allow you to see how each bitwise is calculated and how it changes the register. This is a long program with a very long output. To study it fully, you can access

Note:

This program uses *usingnamespacestd;* to simplify the program.It would be good practice to omit the namespace and declare each *cout* and *bitwise* object separately.

C

The last binary operators we will discuss are assignment operators. **Assignment operators** are used for assigning value and dynamically changing values. In principles of programming, we talked about programs needing to be as efficient as possible while using a few instructions as possible. Advanced assignments operators combine with equal assignments and other various operations to reduce lines of code. They are all **atomic operations**, meaning they allow programmers to manipulate stored values within variables, and reassign them. Below is a list of common assignment operators (Prabhu, 2018):

" = ": Equal assignment operator assigns the value on the right to thevariable on the left.

" += ": Operator for atomic addition, used to combine the ' + ' and ' = ',

operators. This operator **adds** the value of the variable on the left to thevalue on the right. Then it saves the result to the variable on the left.

For example,

x += y would be a shorter way of writingx = x + y

without having to use a separate arithmetic operator."

" -= ": The atomic subtraction used to combine the ' - ' and ' = '

operators. This operator **subtracts** the value of the variable on the leftfrom the value on the right. Then it saves the result to the variable onthe left.

" *= ": Operator for the atomic multiplication, used to combine the ' * ' and ' = '

operators. This operator multiplies the value of the variable on the leftwith the value on the right and saves the result to the variable on the left.

$\neq$

": The atomic division operator is a combination of '⁄'and ' ' operators. This operator divides

the value of the variable on the left by the value

on the right and saves the result to the variable on the left.

For example, x

$\neq$ y would be a shorter way of writing

$$x = \frac{x}{y}$$

without having to use a separate arithmetic operator.

Note: There are also bitwise atomic assignment operations: "

= ", "| = ", and " $\wedge =$ ". We will focus on the arithmetic-atomic

functions for now.

Let's create an assignment operator routine program to see how theseassignment operations work. Follow these steps:

Open a new IDE workspace

Declare and initialize our variableint a = 10;

Print an explanation of the program and the starting value

Note: When making programs that print, always make them easy toread! Make sure your program can explain itself.

Atomically add 10 and print the result

Atomically subtract 10 from our variable and print the result

Atomically multiply 10 and print the result

Atomically divide our variable by 10 and print the resultHere is how it looks:

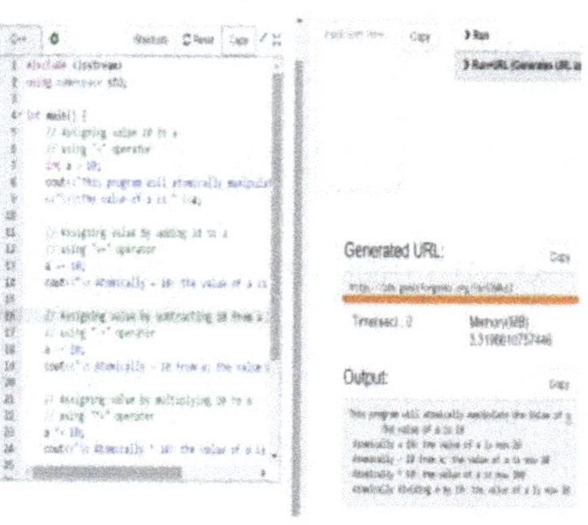

Assignment Routine

This screenshot is a successful run of our assignment routine program. This program has a sequential output, which means that each instruction impacts the result of the next instruction. This means

if we were to change the order of the atomic operations applied to that the output would be different. To study it fully, you can access it on our saved workspace using this URL:
https://ide.geeksforgeeks.org/Fbc63b0u1E

These binary assignment operators combine assignments and arithmetic functions. They work well when controlling loops and conditional statements, too. Atomic assignment operators are closely related to unary arithmetic operators. Both are frequently used to control loops. Let's take a look at unary operations.

Unary Operations

Before we discuss unary operations, let's look at code that uses them.

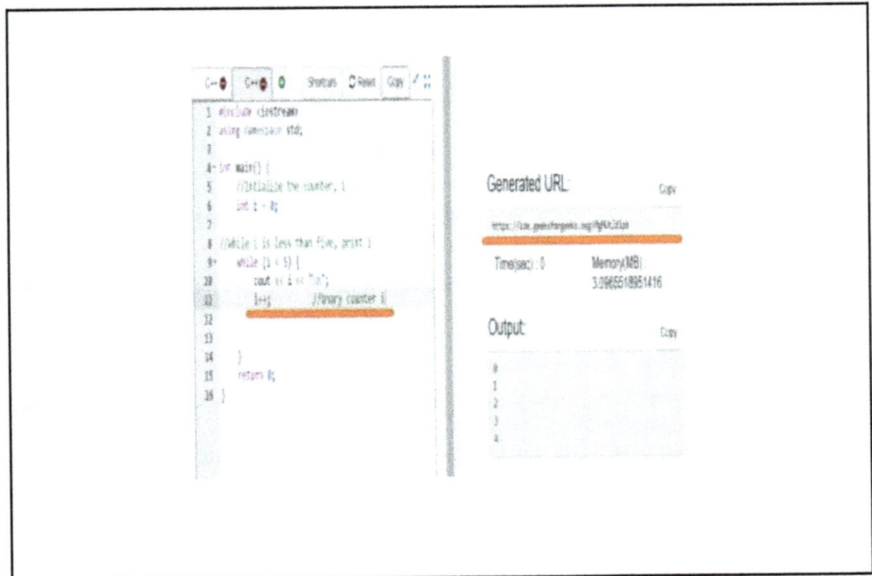

While Loop featuring a Unary Operator

This screenshot is of a simple while loop that prints the value of the Counter, will cause an error as the while loop would not be able to advance. Wewill talk about loops extensively in the decision making chapter. To study it fully, you can access it on our saved workspace using this URL: https://ide.geeksforgeeks.org/MgMUtZdlpb

i. The unary operation performsi

= 1 + i for each iteration untili
= 5
and the while loop ends. Omitting
i ++

The *i* = 1 + i is the same as *i++*. Using the unary form makes the code neater because it precludes the + arithmetic operator and the =assignment operator. We can also use an atomic addition operator tocomplete the code: *i+=1* is the same as *i++*. But a format like that would require the compiler to store and operate on an additional operand.

Unary operators are there to simplify code by only having one operand. Remember, unary operators are those operators that use one operand. Here are some of the other examples of unary operators (Kumar, 2017) :

" **++** ": Increment operator used to increase the value of an integer by 1. It can be placed in front of a variable to increment the value immediately or after to temporarily save the value before increment.

" -- ": Decrement operator used to decrease the value of an integer by 1. Similar to the increment, programmers can also implement pre-decrement and post-decrement instructions.

" - ": Unary minus operator that is used to change the sign of a variable or argument. Performing a unary minus operation on anegative integer will make it positive and vice versa.

"!": NOT operator is used to reverse the Boolean logical state of anoperand. For example, if a variable has a Boolean value of false, !x will be true

"": Address of operator that is used to point to the address of avariable.

Let's make a unary operator routine to see how the pre- and post-instructions work. Follow these instructions:

Open a new IDE workspace

Declare and initialize our variable and a bufferint a = 10, buf

Print an explanation of the program and the starting value

Calculate a post-increment equal to the buffer and print theresult

Calculate a post-decrement equal to the buffer and print theresult

Calculate a pre-increment equal to the buffer and print theresult

Calculate a pre-decrement equal to the buffer and print the result

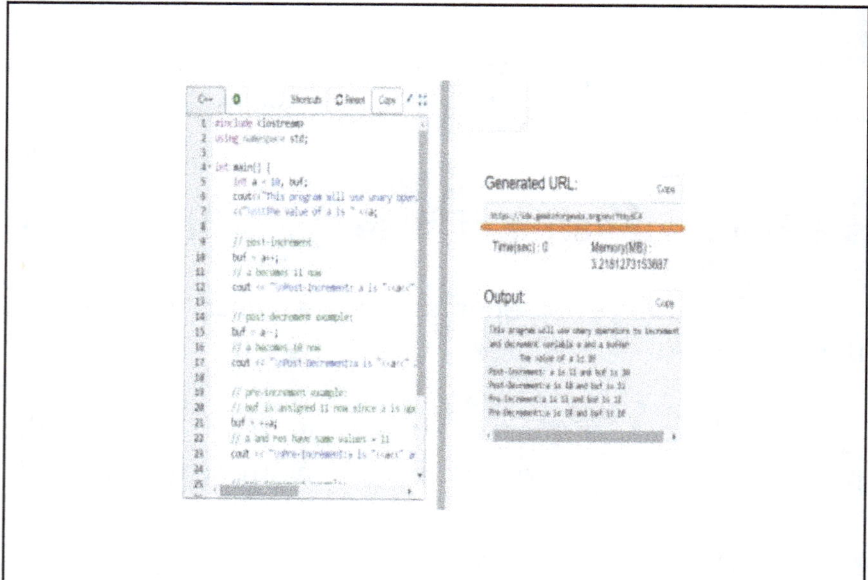

Unary Operator Routine with Post- and Pre-Operations

This screenshot is of our unary operator routine program. To studyit fully, you can access it on our saved workspace using this URL: https://ide.geeksforgeeks.org/mvcYtky6C4

The program operates on *a* and while it calculates, it stores the valuein a buffer we can observe. Comparing *a* with the buffer, the post- operation delays changing the value of a; in contrast, pre-operations change the value immediately.

On top of all this, we have the ***sizeof***() operator. It looks like afunction but it is categorized as an operator. It checks the size of an object and returns the size in bytes.

Recall our conversation about bit streams. What I didn't say is that they are often divided into a group of 8. One byte is a single 8-bit stream that can present 255 numbers. In our bitwise routine, our registers were 1 byte long, that was because we were working with numbers that were less than 255.

Let's write a program that can get the size of an array using ***sizeof***(). Here we go:

Open a new C++ IDE workspace

Declare and initialize our array

```
arr[] = {1,2,3,4,7,98,0,12,35,99,14}
```

Print an explanation of the program and the array

Note: To print the array you will have to create a for loop. We will discuss for loops in the next chapter. For now, just use these lines ofcode:

```
for(constautoe:arr){
```

$$\text{cout} << \text{"["} << e << \text{"]"};$$

$$\}$$

Calculate the size of the array

$$\text{intarsize} = \text{sizeof(arr)}/\text{sizeof(arr[0])}$$

Print the size of the array

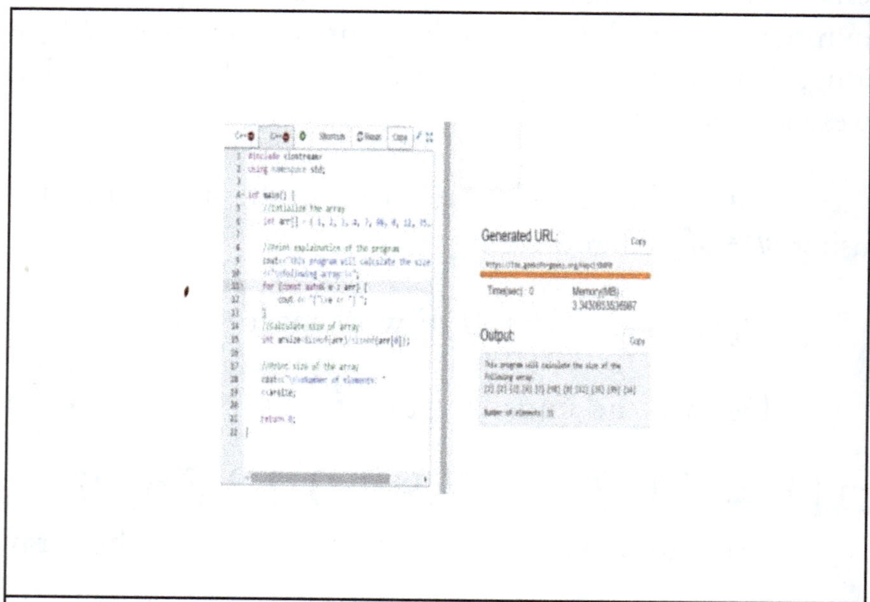

Array Size Reporting Program

This screenshot is of our array size reporting program. We encourage you to compare your result to ours. To study it fully, you can access it on our saved workspace using this URL:

That was a good example of two unary operations: *sizeof()* and the address pointer &. The *for(){}* loop we used to print the array is called a copy constructor call. **Constructor copy calls** consist of a *for()* loop with an index variable, an *Addressof* operator, and a container object with an index. The copy constructor sets up [0]: [the size of arr] by using the *Addressof* pointer to automatically deduce the [size of arr] and print its contents. In simple words, a copy constructor uses *Addressof* to reduce the size of the program.

The *sizeof()* operator is an objective operation and it uses a single operand, the arr array object. They both have disadvantages and advantages. The *sizeof()* operator uses one operand and is easier to spot without esoteric memory registers. The call combination had to use an additional object (*e*), to print the array but it would have done with less incrementing operators. We are going to discuss loops and decision making features of C++ in more detail in the next chapter. For now, let's turn our attention to ternary operators.

121

Ternary Operators

C++ only has one ternary operator. **Ternary operators**, also called conditional operators, take 3 or more operands – they are Boolean logic-based operators. The result is always determined by whetheror not the first expression is true, then the second will be evaluated;if the first expression is false, the third expression will be evaluated. If you recall our *if()...else* statement in the relational program routine, it had three parts: an initial expression that the function evaluates, an expression it evaluates if the initial expression is true, and an else statement which is evaluated when the initial expression is not true. Conditional operators have the same components as an *if()...else* statement. They are just more compact.

Let's make a program that illustrates these similarities:

Open a new IDE C++ workspace

To use the conditional operator you will have to call the

< bits/stdc ++ .h > library

Print an explanation for the conditional operator

This program will pick the greatest one using two methods: a conditional operator and an statement

We expect a result of 5.

Declare the variable and execute the conditional operatorint arsize=sizeof(arr)/sizeof(arr[0]);

Print an explanation for the 

if(2 > 5) then print 2

else print 5

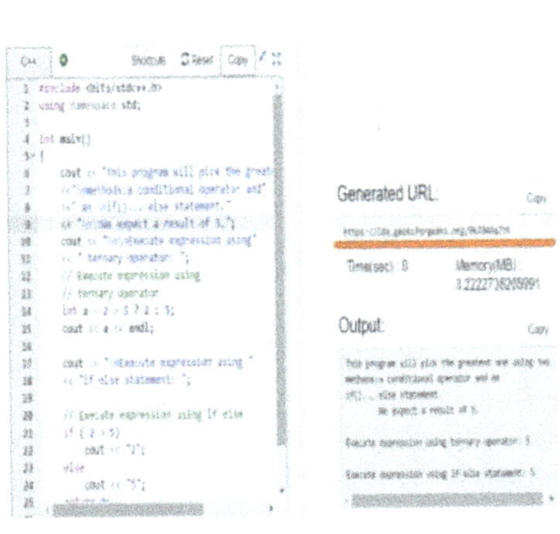

Conditional Operations Demo

This screenshot is of our conditional operations demo. This program has no real practical functionality. However, for our purposes, it does demonstrate the similar structures between conditional operators and statements. To study it fully, we suggest that you access the copy of our saved workspace using this URL: https://ide.geeksforgeeks.org/9kJBAAqJtK.

In this chapter, we looked at 3 types of operators: unary, binary, and ternary. As you have seen, these operators allow programmers to apply powerful aspects of C++. For instance, binary operators allow machines to make logical decisions, compute values, and control processes by changing functions. Unary functions help us shrink and simplify complicated code. Ternary operators allow us to be more succinct in our code. They are all central to making decisions and switching in C++.

CHAPTER 5:

DECISION MAKING IN C++

In this class, we're going to talk about decision-making tools. These tools are like if-else loops. In chapter 4, we saw how operators can be used in logical expressions. When we make decisions, we use these expressions to help us think about them. People write programs for machines that make decisions based on what they want them to do. Decision-making functions and logical expressions make this possible.

This is what happened in Chapter 4. We used a for() loop in a copy constructor to field the array and print all the indices. To make the for() loop work, we used the unary operator Addressof with an auto data type. This meant that we didn't need to make a separate counter for the loop. If you haven't had to start and finish loops yourself, the copy constructor's simplicity isn't as clear as it should be.

Loops

Programmers spend a lot of time automating mundane, repetitive tasks through scripts and routines. What allows scripts and routines to achieve this are loops. As the name suggests, loops repeat the same instructions as long as a certain condition is met ("C++ While Loop," n.d.). Loops are often used to navigate aggregated objects with indiceslike arrays and vectors. For instance, you might write a loop that keeps searching an array until a specific item is found. There are two types of loops: entry-controlled loops and exit loops.

In our unary arithmetic example, we had a **while**() loop with a counter. The counter is an arbitrary variable that is used with a unary operator to increment an indicated expression. It is an example of an entry controlled loop – it tests a condition before it executes code. Let's modify that example into a **while**() loop to explore its components. We will use it to print out "Hello World" 10 times. Follow these instructions:

Open the following IDE C++ workspace: https://ide.geeksforgeeks.org/MgMUtZdlpb

Print explanation of the program This program will number and print 10 lines--

Change the conditional test to $i < 11$

Print "Hello World" 10 times with numbered lines

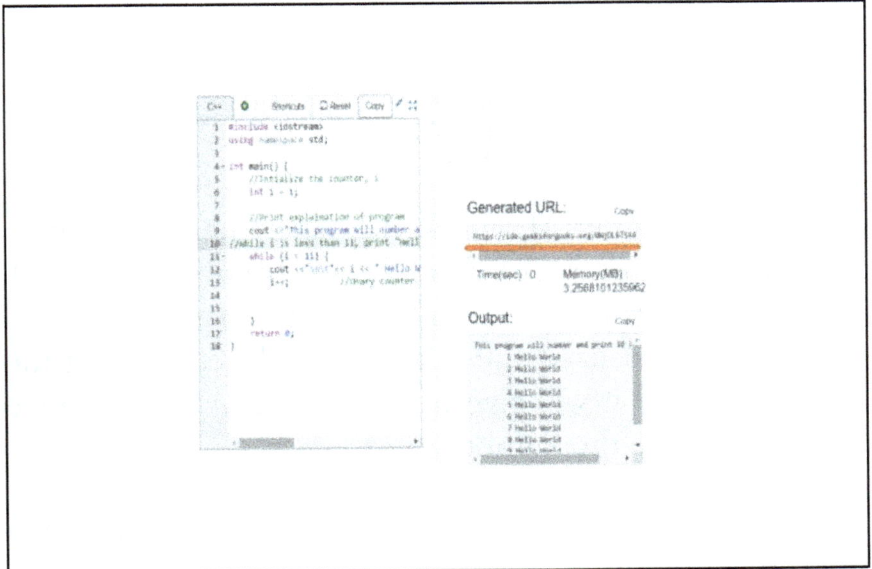

While Loop Demo

This screenshot is of our while loop demo. You can access a copy of our saved workspace using this URL:
https://ide.geeksforgeeks.org/0WjOL6TSh4.

This program shows us how incremental counters work. For it to work, the number must start with 1, not 0. Most people are used to numbers working that way. To do this, we initialized the counter at 1. Yet if weset the condition to 10 it will give us 9 print outs. To get 10 we have to increase the number to 11.

Another example of a controlled loop is the for() loop function; it requires three expressions as inputs (Agarwal, 2017a):

An initialization expression that declares a data type and a variable.This variable can be either a counter or an indexing variable.

true or false

A test expression that produces a Boolean.   If thecondition is true then the for loop will continue to loop its specifiedblock of code.

An update expression that increments the counter or the indexing variable

Let's see how they work by writing a program similar to our **_while_**() loop example. Follow these instructions:

Open the following IDE C++ workspace:
https://ide.geeksforgeeks.org/0WjOL6TSh4

Print explanation of the program

This program will number and print 10 lines of Hello World

Implement the for() loop

for(inti = 1;i < 11;i ++)

Print "Hello World" 10 times with numbered lines

Clean the data of any unneeded code and comments

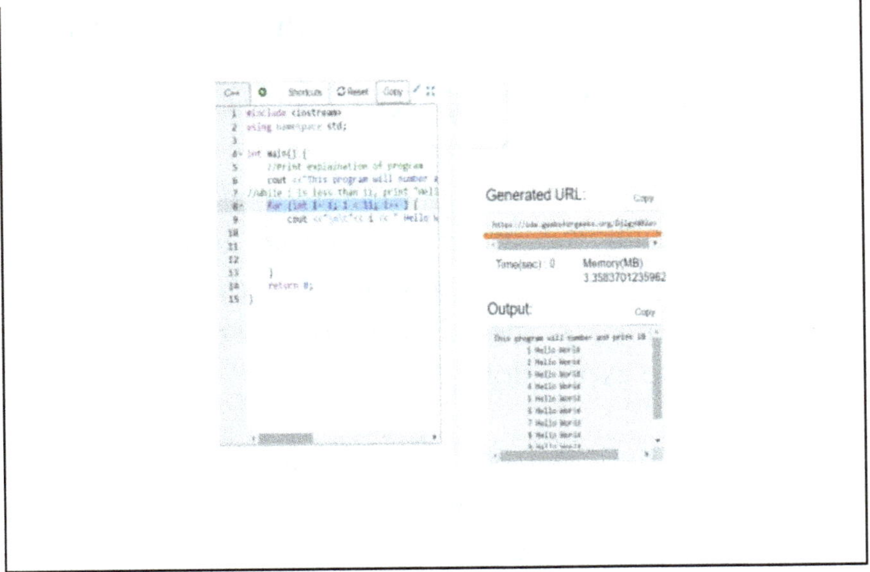

For Loop Demo

This screenshot is of our for loop demo. You can access a copy of oursaved workspace using this URL:https://ide.geeksforgeeks.org/Dj2gyW02av.

Note: Make sure you clean your code of unnecessary lines andupdate your comments. While this does not impact the performanceof your code, it can make things confusing for other programmers on your team that have to implement your code. Do you see a mistake here?

Now that we see how *for*() loops work and how they are constructed, let's look at the copy constructor we used earlier. The expression used for the copy constructor

for(constautoe:arr)

call was:

"E" being the indexing variable and *"arr"* the variable array. We sawthat the *for() loop* needs three expressions to work: the initialization,the test expression, and the update expression.

The copy constructor has an initializing function (*const auto& e*). When you look closely, you can see this expression also works as a test expression, because the & is an Addressof operator that points to *e* which stands for indices in the *arr* array. The : is an operator to break into class. It allows the attributes of the container *arr* array to pass to the *e* variable. The *for()* loop will print the *e* until the end of the array is reached.

The copy constructor call is good for a situation where the size of the container is unknown and you want all items printed out. *For()* loops define the number of iterations that have to take place from the get-go, while copy constructors calls are defined by the size of the container. *While()* loops are best for the situation where the condition can change at any time, during which you want the iterations to stop.

The *do{}…while()* loop is for situations where the *while()* code may impact the test. *Do{}..while()* loops are exit controlled, meaning code is executed until a condition is met. The code is executed at least once before checking the test condition. Think back to that bank security example. The door will always fail-close, receiving a NOT signal, except when there is a fire. Here is how a

do{Keepthedoorslocked}
while(fire = false);

do{}..while loop will look for that:

The door will remain closed as long as fire is not detected. *Do{}..while()* loops are useful for many fail-close systems. Other applications includedata correction in servers where a correction routine is run when an error is detected. Let's code our first do while loop by changing our *while()* program. Follow these instructions:

Open the following IDE C++ workspace: https://ide.geeksforgeeks.org/0WjOL6TSh4

Initialize counter to $inti = 11;$

Implement the do{} code block

Set $while(i < 11);$

Clean the data of any unneeded code and comments

Check the results

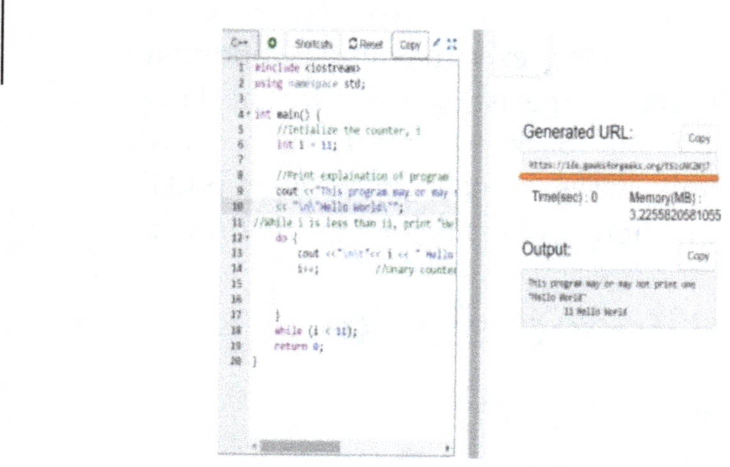

i

< 11 being false for the entire duration of the pro
the do{}

Do While Loop Demo exhibiting an exit controlled loop

This screenshot is of our do while loop demo. You should notice that,despite code block was executed. This is because the loop is an exit control loop: the condition is tested after the code block is executed. The codehas the potential to execute. You can access a copy of our saved workspace using this URL:

https://ide.geeksforgeeks.org/t6zcNK2Wj7.

See how the message was printed despite the conditions being false. You can apply it to data corrections in streams. Many error detection services pause the stream of data and a request for retransmission is sent. A *do{}...while* loop will allow the data stream to continue until an error is detected. These are the types of routines used by YouTube in server buffers. This shows how useful they are in controlling data. For single switching, we would use an *if()...else*.

If()...Else

So far we have used *if()...else* functions in our examples. They are easy to understand and their structure is pretty self-explanatory. An *if()*

...else statement tests a condition and based on the result it executes one block of code or another. They are a combination of two separate distinct statements.

133

You can execute the *if*() function alone but the compiler expects an*else* statement. An *else* statement contains the code that accompanies the *if*() expression. An else statement can never be executed without the *if*() statement.

An *else if*() statement specifies another condition to test. It creates a chain of statements called nested *if-else* statements. If you are testinga lot of conditions, it is best to use a switch which we will discuss in the next section. Let's make our first nested *if-else* statement. Follow these instructions ("C++ | Nested Ternary Operator," 2018):

Open a new IDE C++ workspace

Print an explanation for the conditional operator

This program will go through a sequential list of numbers 2 through 4 and pick the greatest one using a nested if()...else statement

We expect a result of 4.

Implement a nested if-else if(2 > 3) then print 2

elseif(3 > 4) then print 3

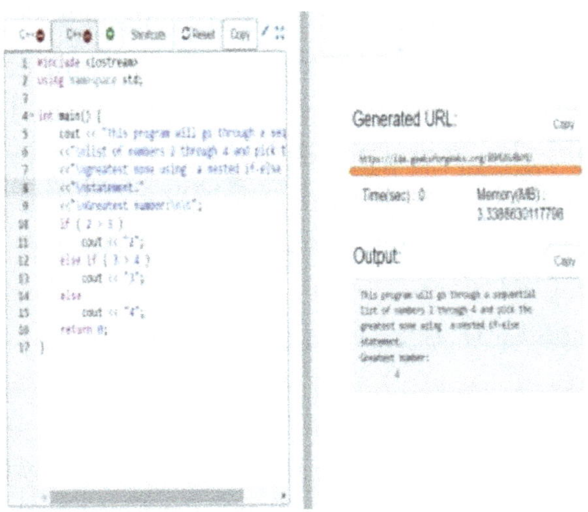

if()...else

statements. Despite us already knowing the answer
if()...else

Nested If-Else Demo

This screenshot is of our nested if-else demo. Just like our other demos, this program has no functionality. However, for our purposes, this is an excellent exercise for implementing and understanding still requires code blocks for each statement. The code blocks should also correspond to the condition in order to create a functional program that fulfills its stated purpose. You can access a copy of our saved   workspace using this   URL: https://ide.geeksforgeeks.org/89MlNvRWYU.

Let's examine the exercise further. The nested *if-else* can be divided into two parts: the *if()* and *else – if()* statement that contains conditions and execution code. You notice that the blocks of code logically follow the state goal of the program, which is to find the largest number. It makes sense to print numbers in ascending order in case we change the conditional statement. Conditions within the *if()* statements and the blocks of code they contain are arranged in a way that allows the program to flow to the answer. For instance, if (2 > 3) is hardcoded to the next nested statement. The structure followed the nested conditional operator deliberately.

Nested Ternary If Else Operator

In the previous chapter, we talked about conditional operators, ternary operators that test conditions and execute an expression based on the results. We said the structure it uses is similar to an *if()...else* statement but more succinct. For instance, an *if*() statement tests a condition and executes one of the two blocks of code depending on theresult of the test. If ()...*else* statements can be nested, and conditional operators can also be nested. Let's compare the structures of both. Follow these steps to participate ("C++ | Nested Ternary Operator," 2018):

If you had closed the nested if-else demo, open up the saved IDE C++ workspace with our program at this URL: https://ide.geeksforgeeks.org/89MlNvRWYU

Print an explanation for the program

This program will go through a sequential list of numbers 2 through 4 and pick the greatest one using two methods: a conditional operator and a nested if()...else statement

We expect a result of 4.

Add a printed notification of the nested if-else

Print a notification for the conditional statement

Add the conditional operator code: declare the variable andexecute the conditional operator

int a = 2 > 3 ? 2 : 3 > 4 ? 3 : 4;

Clean the code of any unnecessary lines and correct anyannotations

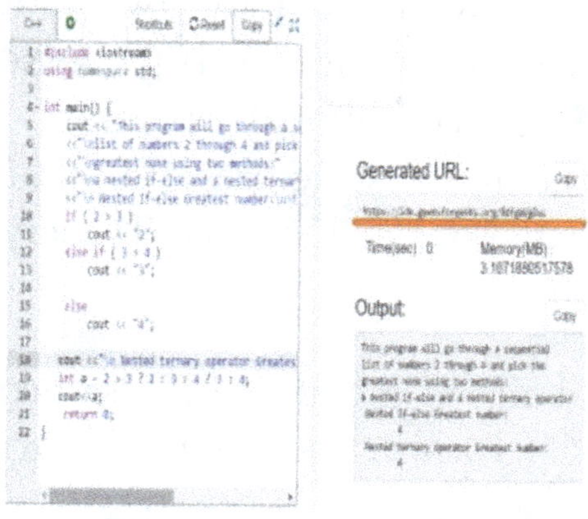

Nested If-Else and Nested Ternary Operation Comparison

This screenshot is of our modified nested if-else demo. We modified our demo by implementing a nested ternary operator for side-by-side comparison. As you may have experienced, the ternary operator was much easier to implement, using fewer statements. You can access acopy of our saved workspace using this URL: https://ide.geeksforgeeks.org/BdfgWVg8uc.

Let's talk about what we have just done there. In our previous discussion, we broke down the nested *if-else* statement into its components and a list of possible results. Even in the case where "2" and "3" were arbitrary values, if-else statements have to list all possibleresults to ensure great functionality regardless of the conditional statements results.

To see how conditional statement results of a nested *if-else match* withcomponents of ternary operator, we have to take a close look at the ternary operator. Here is the syntax:

var

$$= (\text{expression})_1 ? [\text{resultiftrue}]_1 \square \text{expression}$$
$$)_2 ?$$
$$[\text{resultiftrue}]_2 : [\text{resultiffalse}]_2$$

Var is the variable used to print the result. The result of the nested if- else match expression before the ? indicators of the operator. The second expression executes when the first expression is false and corresponds to the *else if* () in the nested if-else. You can already see advantages to the compactness of ternary operators, but by their nature ternary operators are not suited for code blocks. With three or more expressions both get cluttered, so we need something else to handle multiple expressions: the switch statement.

Switch

As I have said, programmers need to strive for efficient, easily understandable code. It makes work easier for you and everyone else. Using switch over *if()..else* is one way you can achieve this, especially in circumstances where we are handling a lot of expressions. Ternary operators reduce lines of code, and it is because of this that they are not suited for situations where the code needs to span more than one line.

Switch statements offer a solution for both problems. Switch statements are multibranch statements that provide a clean way to execute a different block of code on one variable. Here is the syntax (Awasthi, n.d.):

```
switch(n)
  {

  case1 ://codetobeexecutedifn = 1

    break;
  case2 ://codetobeexecutedifn = 2;

    break;


  default://codetobeexecutedifndoesn'tmatchanycases


  }
```

Note: A switch can only evaluate an integer against case numbers. To add the conditional component, you must change the variablewith an operation. The operator must produce an integer.

Let's create a switch demo practice the components

of a switch:

Open a new IDE C++ workspace

Initialize a variable

intx = 2;

Print an explanation of the program

Initialize the switch

switch(x)

Print out "Choice is 1" for case 1

Print out "Choice is 2" for case 2

Print out "Choice is 3" for case 3

Print out "Program Exit" for the default;

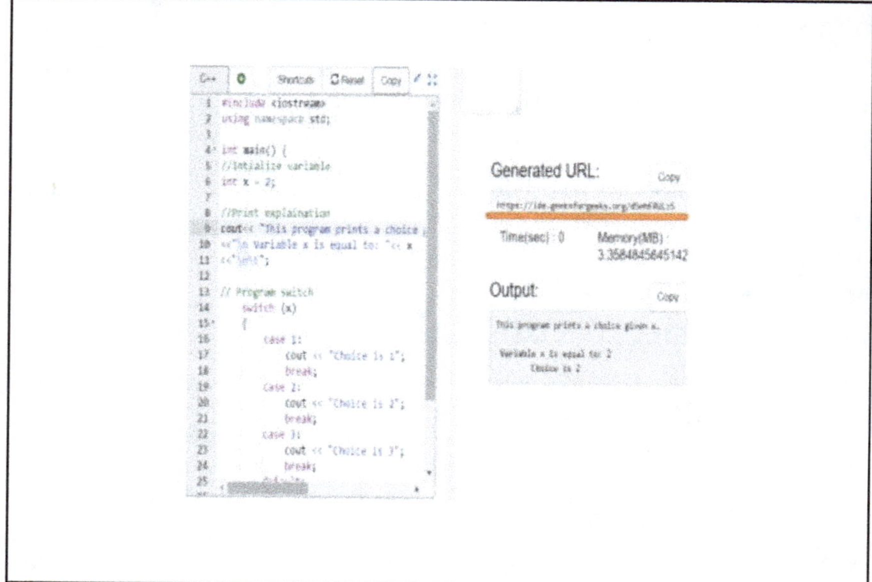

Switch Demo

This is a screenshot of our switch demo. You can access a copy of our saved workspace using this URL: https://ide.geeksforgeeks.org/dSehFXULz5. We highly suggest using this demo to convert one of our previous exercises into a switch. One excellent candidate is our relational routine program. It had **6** if()... else statements! This comes out to 12 different scenarios. How could you convert this program into a switch? Hint: Consider creating a menu for each relational routine using the input function. You can study the relational routine for yourself at this URL: https://ide.geeksforgeeks.org/dFD3cEk85y.

Now that we have seen what decision making functions are and how they work, let's turn our attention to functions and their role in programming.

CHAPTER 6:
CREATING FUNCTIONS

It's a way to figure out what's wrong with a problem and figure out how your code will help fix it. Algorithms get inputs, do things, and then give a result that changes a state. A function is a piece of code that you can use many times without having to write the code again. The code is usually something that does what it's supposed to and can be used again and again. A function is made up of a header and a main body. Here is how the syntax of a function looks:

[datatype]function_name(arguments)
//statements

{

return0;

}

Like you have seen, and like many other programming languages, C++ is mostly just a series of functions, statements, and operators with objects and other data-holding elements for in-between. Everything we have written so far has used the *main()* function which uses syntax similar to the one above. So functions aren't new to you.

Every function must return a data type, just like the *main()* function returns the *int* 0. If a function does not do this, (void) is used as the parameter return type. As you might have guessed, the *return* is the statement that terminates the function.

The inputs that the functions receive are called parameters or arguments. Not all functions will take inputs as we have seen with *main*(); regardless of this, you can still pass parameters into thefunction for it to run. This is how libraries pass objects into *main*().

Create and Call a Function

To begin calling a function, you must declare it and define it before *main*(). This is because C++ executes sequentially. C++ practices take precedence and functions get priority. This is why you must declare them before *main*() so you can call them. They are also called this way because they make code more organized. Once a function is declared, we can define it anywhere outside of *main*()

Let's write a simple printing function so we can appreciate them more. Follow these instructions:

Open a new IDE C++ workspace

Declare your functionvoid myFunction();

Call your function in main ()myFunction()

Define your function outside of main

```
{cout << "Ijustgotexecuted!";}
```

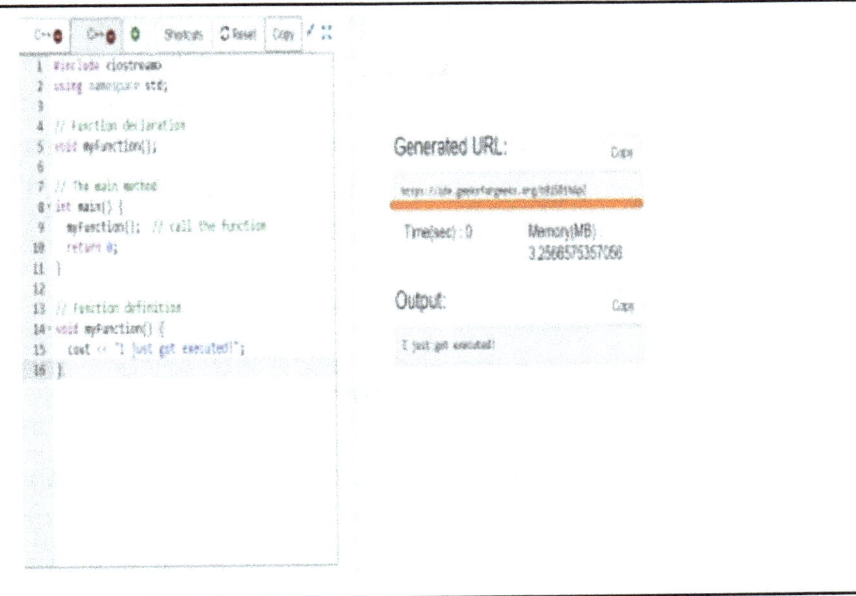

unction Demo

his screenshot is of our function demo. You can access
copy of oursaved   workspace
             using   this   URL:

Separating the declaration and the definition falls under good programming practices. It makes it so you know all defined functions in the code that are available for calling. Having definitions at the bottom makes it easy to parse for errors within functions. Now let's turn our attention to parameter passing.

Parameter Passing

Functions are scripts that are given to the compiler. To complete the task and be useful, these functions need inputs to compute. To remind you, these inputs are called arguments or parameters. Programmers describe parameters differently based on where they originate or appear. Parameters that go into a defined function are

https://ide.geeksforgeeks.org/b9iSDihApZ. If you want more practice, we suggest using this exercise as a template to turn one of our past exercises into a function! Consider our exercise using

```
cin
```

and passing parameters to it. Any function with

```
cout
```

will

do.

called actual parameters. For instance, if you have a summing function called *mySum(x,y)*, when *main()*

passes 2 and 3 into the functions those parameters are actual parameters. Conversely, x and y are formal parameters because they are variables that the data is going to be bound to. This applies to all other parameters before actual parametersare passed. There are two ways to pass parameters to functions ("Functions in C/C++," 2015):

Pass by Value: Values of actual parameters are copied into andstored in the function's formal parameters. Any changes made inside *main*() do not impact the actual parameters that were passed.

Pass by Reference: Both actual and formal parameters refer to the same locations. Therefore, any changes made inside the *main*() function will impact the actual parameters that were passed.

Let's practice parameter passing by writing our own code. Follow theseinstructions:

Open a new IDE C++ workspace

Declare your functionint max(int x, int y)

Call your function in main ()

Initialize two actual variables

inta = 10,b = 20;

Initialize a variable and call the functionint m = max(a, b);

Print the result

149

End main()

Define your function outside of main

This function should use an if() statement to check if x isgreater than y.

If x is greater than y, then return x

Otherwise, return y.

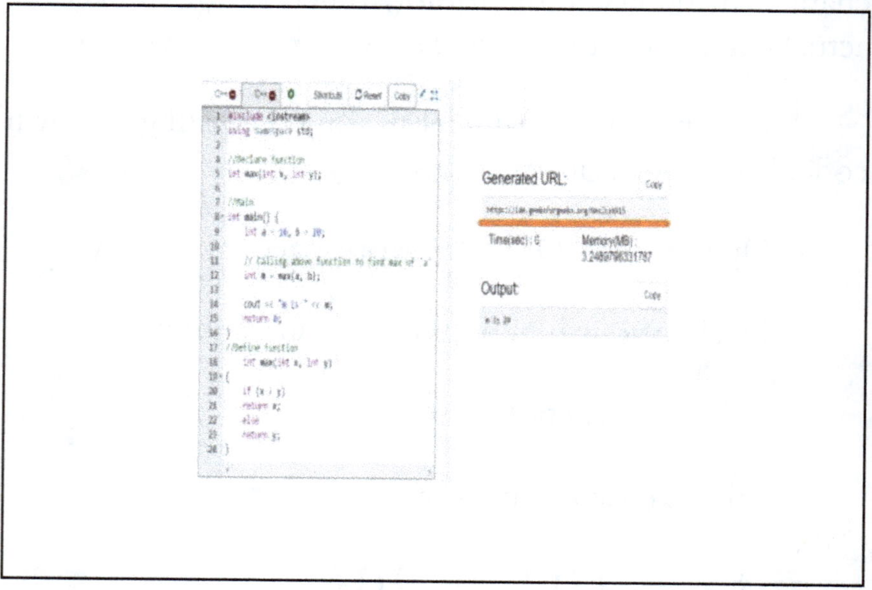

Functions with Parameter Passing

This screenshot is of our function demo. You can access a copy ofour saved workspace using this URL: https://ide.geeksforgeeks.org/NnsZczhX15. If you want more practice,we suggest using this exercise as a template to turn one of our past

exercises into a function! Consider our exercise using and passing parameters to it. We'll discuss how to pass parameters in the next section, but trying it first on your own will help you grasp the concept.

In our example, we have used value passing well. The variables used for *main* (*a,b*) are in a different location than those used in *max*(), (*x,y*). You can see how this can be very useful in larger programs where several complicated computations might take place in *main*(). It is preferred to pass values because it ensures that actual variables remain present until the function is called again.

Using a reference to pass arguments has its own advantages, especially in larger programs. References to pass inessential values may speed up the program and make it responsive. Scripting for automating functions is more likely to use references to pass parameters since automated processes are likely to happen repeatedlyand quickly. These qualities are a selling point for reference-based structures. Let's now turn our attention to condensing and optimizing code.

Function Overloading

All defined objects and classes must have unique names. You cannot run a program that has two variables that have the same name or an error will be thrown. You might have seen this earlier while we're working on our routines and demos, especially when we had to modify a program. So keep this in mind: variables that are declared twice cause errors. But weirdly, multiple functions can have the same name as other functions as long as they have different parameters. This is only allowed in circumstances where the functions return different data types. It is better, given that, to overload a function to return multiple data types. This is what iscalled **function overloading**; a process where programmers combine functions to receive multiple data types. Why? Because it simplifies and consolidates the code. Take a look at the following code ("C++ Function Overloading," n.d.):

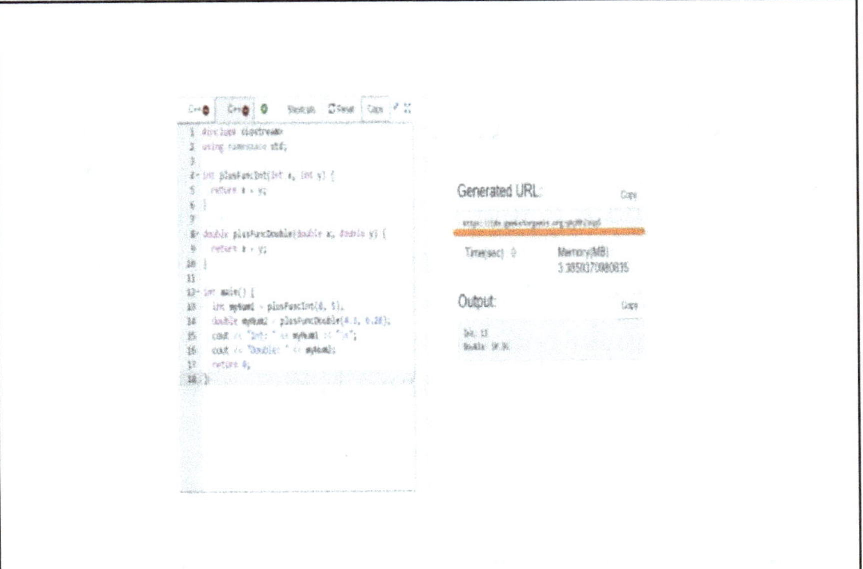

Program without function overloading

You can access a copy of our saved workspace using this URL: https://ide.geeksforgeeks.org/qkpHhZsqq5. The functions are declared and defined at the top of the file so that we can observe them better. You will be using this file to perform function overloading on your own. Remember that you can return to this workspace at any time if your code is damaged during editing.

The program above declares two separate functions that do similar computations. In a big program that is a waste of real estate and it is inefficient. It makes it harder to edit the code since either one of the functions are unlikely to be in the same place in a larger program. Tomake things more efficient, we should consolidate these functions under one name, and "stack" the data types. Here's how you can do this:

Open the saved IDE workspace at the following URL:https://ide.geeksforgeeks.org/qkpHhZsqq5

Change double plusFuncdouble...to double plusFunc...

Call double plusFuncdouble... in place of double plusFunc...

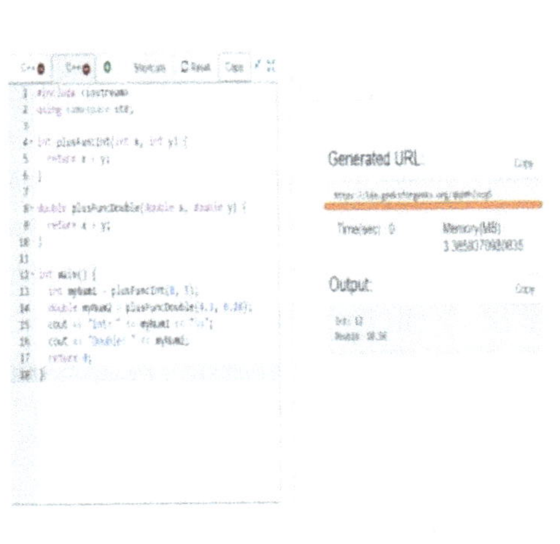

Program function overloading

You can access a copy of our saved workspace using this URL: https://ide.geeksforgeeks.org/e1qLzi3aGo. We kept the functions atthe top of the file for easier editing. This overloading exerciserequires a few small minute detail changes in order for this file to work. Use our workspace to compare your file in the event you get any long-standing errors. Remember that you can return to the original workspace at any time if your code is damaged during

diting. You can access the original workspace at this URL:https://ide.geeksforgeeks.org/qkpHhZsqq5.

When you consolidate similar functions, you clean up your code. It isimportant, especially when you have to debug the code, since the compiler will likely point to functions when errors occur. The compiler does this because it is pointing to multiple libraries in the C++ code. Consolidating and overloading functions ensures that your compiler will have fewer functions to reference, making it easier for you to debug. Keep in mind that C++ is constantly updating so it becomes even easier to work with. New features are constantly added, and libraries are condensed and further organized. So an error is C+++7 would look different than an error in C++14. Updates bring new, easyways to perform mundane tasks. For instance, the copy constructor call combinations are considered more modern for indexing containers such as arrays. To stay updated and reap the benefits of new C++ developments, you have to keep practicing, testing yourself, and asking questions.

CONCLUSION AND FINAL NOTES

Learning how to code is a mental journey that can be fun, exciting, and sometimes frustrating. In the end of this book, we should go over some of the important things we learned. Because of this, they're also going to come with some final thoughts and suggestions that are meant to help you keep growing in this field.

Expanding Your Practice: Preparing Your Coding Environment

We have used an online IDE to make sure everyone has the same experience, so we can all write the same code. Use the Run+URL button to save your work in a different place. You can also save these for later by using your saved IDE workspace and the URLs in this book. Use them as a guide or to fix bad code. I have tried to show you the best ways to code in all of the exercises we did. Make use of the many ways to do things in C++. Don't be afraid to try new things and learn how to do things you want to do. In his book, there aren't any definitive answers to any of the questions. Programming doesn't have that kind of thing. So, come to this book for help and look at other ways to do something. This book has a list of our codes at the top, so you can find them quickly.

There are a lot of programming environments and text editors that can work with the C++ language. Some people will have more than one version of C++. A C++17 computer isn't going to work with a C++14 computer. People who use C++ 14 can understand more of its features because they are easier to understand. This version of C++ is easier for people to understand than the one before it, and this trend is likely to keep going. C++11 is the oldest version of C++ that most people can find in most programming environments.

I want you to set up your own IDE and work on it. It will help you grow more quickly and get used to real-world situations faster, so you can learn faster. We have talked about Code:: In this picture there are blocks for Microsoft and the Mac's Xcode. If you have Linux, there are options that are the same across all of them. Linux is a console-based environment that is very popular with software developers because console-based environments have a lot of built-in features that work with programs.

You can find many distros that have a GUI-based desktop that many people like better. Most of them are open source, which means they can be downloaded and set up for free. CentOS is a free Linux distro that can be used to manage servers. Several parts of Red Hat Enterprise Linux (RHEL) are used by CentOS. It is the best way to learn how to work with Red Hat servers.

Coding Best Practices: Ownership of Learning and Collaboration

In our time together we have seen many techniques and best practices for software development. In the first chapter, we talked about how programs should fulfill their tasks with as little code as possible. Thankfully, with each new version of C++, more ways of doing this are added. The majority of beginner programming coursesteach older, less efficient methods of implementing commonprogramming tasks like parsing arrays, conditional statements, and calling functions. You will find most of these techniques are never used in actual programming situations. Most beginner courses are focused on equipping beginners with a strong grasp of the basics – the foundation of your knowledge is often as important as how you are going to progress. As you grow you will find more efficient ways of solving problems with your code, but this can only happen if you practice and study.

If you want to improve as a programmer you have to take ownership of your learning. Learn pre-development tools like algorithms. It is all about learning to fix problems. There are other pre-developmenttools you can try, like diagraming. Diagraming is good for individuals who are visual learners. All of these are great for growing as a programmer; it does not matter which you choose, as long as pre- developments tools are something you take advantage of.

Turning back to algorithms, more detailed algorithms will explain all sorts of data types required for inputs, outputs, and other data. The advantage of algorithms is that you can use them as a shorthand. You can also annotate and manage your code. These habits will helpkeep your code ordered and coherent to your team members. All these practices will help enhance how you see and think about programs.

Software developers work in teams, with several people working on the same piece of code at the same time. The importance of annotating your code becomes very

159

apparent in such situations.

It also happens that working with others will accelerate your growth. When coding with others you learn from their experience and knowledge. As we have said, C++ has a variety of library objects, statements, and other tools. It is as rich as vocabulary in human languages because there are many ways of doing the same things. Your way of fixing a problem will depend on your ability to seeefficient ways of doing so. But ultimately all programming and software developments are creative endeavors. Working with others will increase your programming "vocabulary" – you will learn from how creatively they fix problems and you will find insights of yourown in the process. You should always keep in mind that everyone can contribute something and what they contribute is heavily influenced by the amount of experience they have. So even if youare new to C++, you still have a unique experience and approach to solving problems that other people don't have because you think differently. That in itself is valuable to any team, particularly if you learn to communicate your ideas well. I highly recommend you use the glossary as one of the ways to help you communicate clearly.

In addition to annotations, it is good practice to make your code as clean as possible. I have demonstrated how to comment lines of code to prevent breaking the code during editing. In your exercises, when you break the code beyond repair, you can always start over from our saved IDEs, or you can simply refresh the browser to start over (this will depend on the state you ran and generated the code). Only generate URLs when you need to save your code, not whileyou are developing.

160

We also stressed the importance of code structure. For instance, we talked about the importance of declaring and defining functions: the best practice is to declare your functions on the top and define them after the main() function. It is similar to declaring integers. The techniques ensure you have an inventory of functions, variables, and objects right at the beginning. It works like an index and can help youavoid definition errors.

Formatting and editing your code of unnecessary lines reduces the possibility of errors during development. You should always update your comments when you make a change. Unformatted code will notimpact performance, the logic of the code will. It is a collaboration courtesy to format your code, not to mention how much easier it makes things for you. Other programmers on your team will be able to implement your code, or even improve it, and they will leavecomments.

But these types of practices are not just good for you. As the world moves forward it is becoming more and more complicated, so it is good for programs to explain themselves to the user. If your programprints, make sure it is easy to read. We have seen how this can be done in this book. Use escape sequences like \n to create new lines and \t to create horizontal table so there is enough whitespace to your code. But as a back-end programmer working with servers and other equipment, you may not have to print out as often as a front- end programmer who serves content to the client. The only users who may need to see your print outs are other technicians andadministrators managing those machines through the terminal. Formatting practices are often underused in backend programming, but it is still a good practice to have. It is valuable to administrators and
161

technicians, who do not have the resources to navigate esoteric compiler-generated errors that programmers are used to when debugging. So a program that is formatted and gives this informationclearly in the terminal or consoles is important.

Take Away: Computer Science Concepts in C++

In addition to programming, we also explored some basic computer science concepts. We looked at the behavior of machines and their language. We talked about how learning programming is like learninga new language: both have syntax and rules that ensure communication is possible. C++ is a back-end server language that is used for managing servers that control oceans of data. Unlike high- level languages like Python, which are more human, C++ wants programmers to be more detailed in their code. Each variable mustbe unique in a function or we will have an error. All functions and statements are case sensitive and have specific rules that governthem. We have implemented many *if()...else* statements and made nested *if-else* statements. We saw that conditional statements like *if()* can be executed without the *else*, but a missing *else* statement can cause an error if the condition is false. And just as a missing verb indicates a sentence is incomplete, *else* statements cannot be implemented without an *if()*.

We saw how computers communicate in binary numbers using logical math. We saw bitwise function work at the bit level, completing logical math computations like

162

AND, OR, and NOT. All the other C++ functions that are object-based must be translated by the compiler into machine language. But *bitwise* functions are faster because they skip that step and communicate directly to the machine. They areoften deployed in competitive programming to make highly agile programs and routines. Outside of competitive programming, bitwise functions have some functionality in managing big data.

The challenge with *bitwise* functions is that they are very difficult for humans to understand because they are binary. To see what computers see we had a brief computer science lesson on binary and binary math. We made a "byte-sized" stream of register with our bitwise routine program and we made dynamic buffers to store bits for bitwise computations. Those virtual buffers and registers are how servers manage terabytes of data. Think about this; our buffers and registers were all one byte long, but a terabyte is

10^{12} times larger than our buffer: 1,000,000,000, bytes. These numbers are small for websites lik YouTube which bases its back - end computing on C ++ . The data that YouTube deals with is astronom In 2018 it was 5.25 zettabytes $(10^{21}$

bytes). It was serving over 3.25 billion hours of content ("How much data does YouTube store? - Quora," n.d.). Bitwise functions give these servers the ability to work with this load without interruption or massive delays. This is one of the best examples of the power of C++ and its ability to handle big complex systems. It is a useful language for programmers to learn. If you visualize these data streams as arrays of 8 slots, it will be easier for you to rationalize many bitwise operators, especially shift operators.

In addition to binary programming, we worked with different kinds of data and explored different aspects of object programming. We did plenty of exercises where we dealt with strings, for example. In fact, we used and deployed strings in every one of our exercises. We saw that strings are also arrays of data, and can be manipulated like objects except in a few ways. Strings have a length, size and can be parsed with various objects in the <string> library. Think of the copy constructor call combination we learned. To parse a container of any type, vector or array, you need a *for*()loop with an **Addressof** operator element. That task has a dedicated function in the

164

<string> library where all you need is the index of the item you are parsing. If there is one thing you should take away from this book it is proficiency in handling strings: breakout escape sequences, handling strings through array indexing, and passing strings to different functions.

We also learned and discussed functionality and design considerations. We talked, for instance, about how and when to use loops. Our bank security example was best illustrated by our exit controlled loop example in a fail-close system. Banks, as we said, should always have their doors locked and closed; they fail-close.

ost events in the bank require doors and exits to fail-close and the only time they should open it in a fire. The system should keep everything in check, where a condition is tested AFTER the routine. The exit control loops are also useful in other areas, like in datacontrol. YouTube does data corrections as a secondary routine of normal operations. This makes sure the system is always running,not hunkered by resend-data requests.

As C++ is a backend-language it has to handle and work with multiple types of data. We have had a brief discussion about this when we spoke of vector-based images as an object class and their other object properties. Photo manipulation software like Photoshop is programmed in C++ where aspects like image manipulation take full use of the program's power. Vectors allow image manipulation without loss of quality, unlike .jped or .png that are arrays of pixels. Vectors like .svg or .pdf use vector containers to describe their pixel locations, which has more class features in C++

that allows preservation of the image.

This book is also meant to be reference, so I encourage you to usethe glossary and the index to review topics. The glossary has all the terms bolded and some of the code snippets we looked at. It also includes the section where the terms are discussed in more detail.

GLOSSARY

Term	Definition	Section
"+",	Binary, arithmetic operation that sumstwo variables. Also used to concatenate stringsin the <string> library	Operation:String Concatenation
"++"	Increment operator used to increase the value of an integer by 1. This unary operator is often used to increase a variablewithin a loop.	Unary Operators
"--"	Unary operator thatdecreases a variable within a loop. This unary operator is often used to increase a variable within a loop.	Unary Operators
Arithmetic Operator **"-"**,	Binary operator that subtracts one operand from another	Arithmetic Operators

Unary Operator "-",	Unary minus operator that is used to change the sign of a variable or argument. Performing a unary minus operation on a negative integer will make it positive and vice versa.	Unary Operators
"-="	The atomic subtraction used to combine the '-' and '=' operators. This operator first subtracts the current value of the variable on the left from the value on the right. It then assigns the result to the variable on the left. For example, x-=y would be a shorter way of writing x=x-y without having to use a separate arithmetic operator.	Assignment Operators

Binary Operator "!",	Binary logical "NOT" operator that returns a Boolean true if the conditions in consideration are not satisfied. If one of the conditions is true, then it returns a Boolean false.	Logical Operators
"!",	NOT operator is used to reverse the Boolean logical state of an operand. For example, if a variable x has a Boolean value of false, !x will be true.	Unary Operators
"!="	"Not-Equal" operator that also checks whether two given operands are equal or not. However, this operator returns a Boolean true if the operands are not equal and returns false if the operands are equal.	Relational Operators

"*"	Binary operator thatmultiplies two operands. The order of the operands does not matter.	Arithmetic Operators
"*="	Operator for the atomic multiplication, usedto combine the '*' and '=' operators. This operator first multiplies the current value of the variable on the left to the value on the right and then assigns the result to the variable on the left. For example, x*=y would be a shorter way of writing x=x*y without having to use a separate arithmetic operator.	Assignment Operators
"/"	Binary division "forward slash" operator that divides the first operand into thesecond.	Arithmetic Operators

"/="	Atomic division operator is a combination of '/' and '=' operators. This operator first divides the current value of the variable on the left by the value on right and then assigns the result to the variable on the left. For example, x/=y would be a shorter way of writing x=x/y without having to use a separate arithmetic operator.	Assignment Operators
"\?" **Escape Sequence**	Used for questionmarks.	Using Escape Sequences
"\'" **Escape Sequence**	Used for singlequotes.	Using Escape Sequences
"\"" **Escape Sequence**	Used for doublequotes.	Using Escape Sequences
"\\" **Escape Sequence**	Used for backslashes.	Using Escape Sequences
"\f" **Escape Sequence**	Stands for "form feed" and is used to go to the next"page".	Using EscapeSequences
Escape Sequence **"\n"**	Stands for "line feed" and is used togo to the next line.	Using Escape Sequences

Escape Sequence "\t"	Stands for "horizontal tab" and adds 5 spaces horizontally.	Using EscapeSequences
Escape Sequence "\v"	Stands for "verticaltab" and is used for spacing in vertical languages.	Using Escape Sequences
Unary Operator "&"	Address of operatorthat is used to point to the address of a variable.	Unary Operators
Binary Operator "&",	Bitwise AND that takes two numbers as operands and does AND on everybit within the stream of the two numbers. The result stream of AND is 1 only if both bits are 1.	Bitwise Operators

Operator	Description	Category
"&&"	Binary logical "AND" operator thatreturns a Boolean true when both the conditions in consideration are satisfied. Otherwise, itreturns false.	Logical Operators
"%"	Binary modulus operator that returns the remainder from dividing the first operand into thesecond.	Arithmetic Operators
"^"	Bitwise XOR that takes two numbers as operands and does XOR on everybit within the stream of the two numbers. The result stream of XOR is 1 if the two bits are different.	Bitwise Operators

"+="	Operator for atomicaddition, used to combine the '+' and'=' operators. This operator first adds the current value ofthe variable on the left to the value on the right. It then stores the result to the variable on the left. For example, x+=y would be a shorter way of writing x=x+y without having to use a separate arithmetic operator.	Assignment Operators
"<"	"Less-than" operator that checks whether thefirst operand is lessthan the second operand. If so, thisoperator returns a boolean true. Otherwise, itreturns false.	Relational Operators

"<<"	Left shift operator that takes two numbers and left shifts the bits of thefirst operand. The second operand is used to determine the number of places to shift.	Bitwise Operators
"<="	"Lesser-than or equal-to" operator that checks whether the first operand is less than or equal to thesecond operand. If so, this operand returns a Boolean true. Otherwise it returns false.	Relational Operators
"="	Equal assignment operator, used to assign the value onthe right to the variable on the left.	Assignment Operators

"=="	"Equal" operator that checks whether two givenoperands are equal. If the operands are equal, it returns a Boolean "true", if not it returns false.	Relational Operators
">"	"Greater-than" operator that checks whether thefirst operand is greater than the second operand. If so, this operator returns a Boolean true. Otherwise, it returns false.	Relational Operators
">="	"Greater-than or equal-to" operator that checks whether the first operand is greater than or equal to thesecond operand. If so, this operand returns a Boolean true. Otherwise, it returns a Boolean false.	Relational Operators

">>"	Right shift operatorthat takes two numbers and right shifts the bits of thefirst operand. The second operand is used to determine the number of places to shift.	Bitwise Operators
"|"	Bitwise OR that takes two numbers as operands and does OR on every bit within the stream of two numbers. The result stream of OR is 1 if any of the twobits is 1.	Bitwise Operators
"||"	Binary logical "OR"operator that returns a Boolean true when one (or both) of the conditions in consideration are satisfied. If none ofthe conditions are satisfied, it returns false.	Logical Operators

	Bitwise NOT operator that takes one number and switches the state of all the bits (1s to 0s, 0s to 1s).	Bitwise Operators
"~"		
"bool" Keyword	Datatype keyword that is short for "Boolean" and stores values with two states: true or false. Has a size of 1 byte. these values can be expressed as either "0/1" or "false/true" with a manipulator.	Basic Data Types
"boolalpha/noboolapha" Manipulator	Input-Output manipulator that switches between using "0/1" to "false/true" for Boolean values.	Using Endl: Input/Output Manipulators

"char" Keyword	Data type keyword that is short for "character" and stores single characters regardless of their capitalization. Has a size of 1 byte. Char values are surrounded by single quotes.	Basic Data Types
"cout" object	C++ programming object part of the <iostream> library that allows a program to print out values and text using the "<<" operator. This object must be defined with a datatype, usually "std".	Using Cout

179

"double" Keyword	Data type keyword that is used to storenumbers with decimals with 15 decimal digits. Has a size of 8 bytes. This data type canhold more decimalnumbers and is preferred for mathematical calculations.	Basic Data Types
"else"	Statement is used to specify a code inthe event that its accompanying if() expression is false. Else cannot be used without if ().	Loops
"endl" Manipulator	Input-Output manipulator that outputs "\n" and flushes the outputstream.	Using Endl: Input/Output Manipulators
"ends" Manipulator	Input-Output manipulator that outputs "\0" [zero].	Using Endl: Input/Output Manipulators

"float" Keyword	Keyword data type that stores numberswith decimals with 7 decimal digits. Has a size of 4 bytes. This data type is preferred forholding monetary numbers.	Basic Data Types
"flush" Manipulator	Input-Output manipulator that flushes the outputstream.	Using Endl: Input/Output Manipulators
"get_money" Manipulator	Input-Output manipulator that receives an input as a monetary value. This manipulator works in C++11 only and may cause errors in outdated C++ programming environments.	Using Endl: Input/Output Manipulators

181

"get_time" **Manipulator**	Input-Output manipulator that receives an input as a date/time value according to a specified format. This manipulator works in C++11 only and may cause errors in outdated C++ programming environments.	Using Endl: Input/Output Manipulators
"int" **Keyword**	Data type keyword that is short for "integer" and stores whole numbers. Has a size of 4 bytes. This keyword includes positive and negative integers.	Basic Data Types

| **"put_money" Manipulator** | Input-Output manipulator that formats and outputsa monetary value.

This manipulatorworks in C++11 only and may cause errors in outdated C++ programming environments. | Using Endl: Input/Output Manipulators |
| **"put_time" Manipulator** | Input-Output manipulator that receives an input as a date/time value according toa specified format.

This manipulatorworks in C++11 only and may cause errors in outdated C++ programming environments. | Using Endl: Input/Ouput Manipulators |

"quoted" Manipulator	Input-Output manipulator allowsyou to insert and extract quoted strings with embedded spaces. This manipulator works in C++14only.	Using Endl: Input/Output Manipulators
"showbase/n oshowbase" Manipulator	Input-Output manipulator specifically for mathematical outputs that controls whether aprefix is used to indicate a numericbase.	Using Endl: Input/Output Manipulators
"showpos/n oshowpos" Manipulator	Input-Output manipulator that controls whether the "+" sign is usedto indicate non-negative numbers.	Using Endl: Input/Output Manipulators

"uppercase/ nouppercase "Manipulator	Input-Output manipulator that controls whether uppercase characters are usedwith some output formats.	Using Endl: Input/Output Manipulators
"using namespace std;" Statement	Line of code frequently used to unilaterally declarethe "std" datatype for iostream library objects and manipulators. This unilateral declaration makesthe code easier to see. However, thisis discouraged outside of practicebecause it can make string handling ill-definedin programs, thus, causing errors thatare difficult to mitigate. Exercisesin this book will avoid using this statement.	Omitting Namespace

185

[string_name].length() Attribute	Coding syntax for calling the "length"string object attribute .	String Objects: Length() Attribute
Actual Parameters	Parameters cominginto a defined function.	Parameter Passing
Algorithm	An organizational tool used to plot outthe aspects of a program including (1) data in, if applicable, (2) operations performed on declared variables, and (3) the result ofrunning the program.	Principles of Programming
Arithmetic operators	Binary and unary operations that areused to perform common mathematical operations.	Arithmetic Operators
Assembly language	Describes a low- level programming language that requires a compilerto convert it into machine code.	Chapter 1: Settingup a C++ Development Environment

Assignment Operators	Used to assign a value to a variable and change valueson the fly, reducingthe number of instructions in a program.	Assignment Operators
Atomic Operations	Operations that combine assignments withother operations. Atomic operations allow programmersto manipulate a value stored withina variable and reassign it immediately.	Assignment Operators

Base-10	Number system used by human beings assign place value to numerals. Base-10 is also known as the decimal system because a digit's value in a numberis determined by where it lies in relation to the decimal point. The value is multiplied by a base power of 10, where each point away from theleft of the decimal is$10^{\wedge}(n+1)$ and each point to the right of the decimal is$10^{\wedge}(n-1)$.	Bitwise Operators
Binary Number System	See Base-2	Bitwise Operators
Binary Operator	Classification of operators that execute with twooperands.	Chapter 4: Operations in C++

188

Bitwise Operators	Logic operators thatoperate on numbers at the binary level.	Bitwise Operators
Bluefish	A free software advanced text editor with a varietyof tools for programming in general and the development of dynamic websites.	Setting up the TextEditor
Byte	Measurement of data composed of 8bits. A byte can represent up to 225numbers (0b 1111111).	Unary Operators
C++14	Advanced version of C++ that makes this version slightly more intelligible for humans to programin. "Standard C++" usually refers to C++11, also knownas C++0x.	Chapter 1: Settingup a C++ Development Environment.
CentOS	A free, community-supported. Linux distribution operating system	Linux Compiler Installation

	that is functionally compatible with Red Hat EnterpriseLinux (RHEL).	
Code	See Executable file	Chapter 1: Settingup a C++ Development Environment
Code::Blocks	A free open sourceIDE designed for C++. This IDE supports many C++compilers includingGCC, Clang, and Visual C++ in Microsoft. This IDE can program in C++, C, and Fortran.	Windows IDE Installation
Command-Line Interface (CLI)	Method of interacting with a computer programwhere the user controls the program with entering lines of code.	Setting up a Text Editor

Comments	Lines of code that are ignored by the compiler and indicated by a double slash at the beginning of the line in C++. Comments are used to annotatecode and leave notes to guide other programmers studying your code.	Overview of C++Syntax
Compiled Language	See Low-LevelLanguage	Chapter 3
Concatenation, String	A common programming feature that allows programmers to dynamically controltext by fielding content from a source and servingit within their program. In C++ String Concatenation is done through "+", an arithmetic operator.	Operation:String Concatenation

Conditional Operator	Boolean logic based operator withthree operand expressions. The outcome of the conditional operatordepends on the firstexpression.	Ternary Operators
Conditional Short-Circuit	When program developers use logical operators and conditional statements to control how a program behaves.	Logical Operators
Copy Constructor Call	Method of searching and printing indexes. Consists of for() loop with an index variable with an Addressof operator,and a container object with an index such as an array.	Unary Operators

Counter	An arbitrary variable that is used in conjunctionwith an arithmetic unary operator to incrementally loop an indicated expression.	Loops
Data	Operands, or thevarious kinds of data that the functions and statements are acting on	Overview of Syntax
Data Type	Attribute of a variable which tells the compiler or interpreter how the programmer intends to use the data. Common datatypes include real numbers, integers, and "true-false" Boolean variables.	Chapter 3

Debugging	Process of locationand removing computer program errors and abnormalities, also known as "bugs." As a general rule, smaller, modularized codethat calls on functions is easierto debug than larger files.	Overview of Syntax
Decimal Number System	See Base-10	Bitwise Operators
do {}...while() Loop	Exit controlled loop that tests a single condition and loopsa block of code untilthe condition is met.	Loops

else if()	Conditional statement combination usedto nest conditionalif()... else statements. Programmers are advised to use a switch if there arenumerous conditions to test.	Loops
Escape Sequence	Special in-string character combinations that are used to represent certain special characterswithin strings and character streams. Escape sequencesallow programmersto include symbols in strings without confusing the compiler.	Using Escape Sequences
Executable File	List of instructions that are used toperform the operations of a program.	Chapter 1

File Extension	File suffix that informs the code compiler what language the executable file is in. The C++ language is indicated by ".cpp" or ".hpp" extensions.	Chapter 1
First Principal of Programming	A program must be designed to complete a task in the smallest number of functions possible. This principle reduces overhead and increases performance of a program.	Principles of Programming
for() Loop	Entry controlled loop that has three inputs: an initialization expression, a test expression and an update expression. The for loop will execute its block of code until the test expression reports false.	Loops

Formal Parameters	Variables used to define the initial arguments, and any arguments in the function before theactual parameters are passed.	Parameter Passing
Function	A block of code thattakes inputs to perform an action and runs when called.	Chapter 6: Creating...
Function Overloading	Programming technique of consolidating codethrough stacking several data typesonto one function.	Function Overloading
Functionality	How program features and utilities can be implemented in acode to achieve aspecific result.	Chapter 4: Operations in C++

Functions	Code that encapsulates instructions that may take inputs and output some result. Every function "[function-name]()", where [function_name] issome arbitrary function, is always followed by curly brackets {} and every explicitly stated instruction within the curly brackets will be executed by thecompiler.	Overview of Syntax
Gedit	Free, open-source, general-purpose text editor that includes tools for editing source codeand structured text such as markup languages.	Linux Compiler Installation

getline() function	C++ function from the <string> librarythat extracts all characters from aninput string into a string array.	Cin and getline() function
GNU Collection Compiler (GCC)	An open source compiler system produced by the GNU Project supporting various programming languages. GCC is a key component ofthe GNU toolchain and is the standardcompiler for most Linux projects.	Linux Compiler Installation
Graphical user Interface (GUI)	Method of interacting with a computer program that allows users tointeract with graphical icons andvisual indicators such as secondary notation instead of inputting commands.	Setting up Text

Header File Library	Lines that start with the pound sign (#) that are used by the compiler to call library functions.	Overview of Syntax
if() else Statement	Conditional statement functioncombination that tests a single condition and executes explicitlystated blocks of code based on theresults of the test.	Loops
if()... else statement	A nested function that executes all instructions within its curly brackets "{}" given a specified condition is met. Otherwise, itexecutes the items with the enclosed else {} statement. These statementsalways deploy a relational operandto test the condition.	Relational Operators

Integrated Development Environment (IDE)	Programming environment usedto write code, testfor errors and translate a program.	Chapter 1
Linux distribution (distro)	An operating system made froma Linux kernel based software	Linux Compiler Installation

	collection and package management system for installingadditional software.	
Logic Gates	Physical electronic circuits that have one or more inputs while only having one output. AND gates only pass a "1" when all inputs are "1"; OR gates pass a "1" as their output when they receive a "1" at any of their inputs; NOTgates pass a "1" when they receive a "0" at their input.	Logical Operators
Logical Operators	Binary operators used in combination with the relational operators combine two or more conditions to describe a specificconstraint.	Logical Operators

| Loops | Function that execute a block ofcode as long as a specified conditionis reached | Loops |
| Low-Level Language | A programming language that closely follows a computer's instruction set | Chapter 2 |

	architecture— commands ctions in the language map to processorinstructions. educes the overhead for g the program as the ler takes less resources to te low-level languages into ne code.	
Machine Language	Coding languagethat is directly compiled and executed by a CPU. See "AssemblerLanguage"	Chapter 1
Manipulator, Input/Output	Helper functions within the C++ iostream library that make it possible to control input/output streams using the " <<" operator or the ">>" operator.	Using Endl: Input/Output Manipulators

Notepad ++	Text editor and source code editor for use with Microsoft Windows.	Setting up Text
Object	A general computing term thatdescribes a methodthat the computer	First Program: Output and BasicStrings

	uses to managedata.	
Operand	Operation component thatdescribes the value, object, orvariable being operated on.	Note: Operand...
Operations	Features such as control loops that implement decision-making inprograms.	Chapter 4: Operations in C++
Operator	Operation component that describes the symbol indicating the sort of operation being carried out. Operators are described by how many operands they can operate onat a time: unary, binary, and ternary.	Note: Operand...

| **Organization Identifier** | Proprietary Apple naming convention that is used to create a unique ID for programs across various Apple databases: the Apple Developer Website,and iCloud Container, iTunes connect portal in the Appstore. The | Mac Installation | IDE |

	organization identifier is used asthe first argument of a "reversed domain" that ensures that all developed projectscan be streamlined into the proprietarymacOS framework.	
Parameter Pass by Reference	Both actual and formal parametersrefer to the same locations. Therefore, any changes made inside the main() function will impact the actual parameters that were passed.	Parameter Passing
Parameter Pass by Value	Values of actual parameters are copied into and stored in the function's formal parameters. Any changes made inside main() doesnot impact the actual parametersthat were passed.	Parameter Passing

Red Hat Enterprise Linux(RHEL)	A commercial Linux distribution developed by Red Hat for the commercial market.	Linux Compiler Installation> Note: there are many distributions…
Register	An array of binary storage where each	

	bit gets its own place in the array. Registers are usedto calculate bitwiseoperators.	Bitwise Operators
Relational Operators	Binary operators that are used to compare two values and return aboolean response.	Relational Operators
Script	Supplementary list of commands executed by certain programs or scripting engines.	Chapter 6: Creating...

See Base-2	Number system used by machines to calculate computations. Also known as the binary number system. binary numbers are represented as a stream of bits, where each singular bit can be one of the two states: 1 or 0. The position of the 1 bit in the stream determines the value of the number.	Bitwise Operators
Server-side programming	Writing code that negotiates and delivers content to a dynamic, or changing website.	Mac IDE Installation

	C++ is, majorly, a server side language.	
Service Level Agreement (SLA)	Term in IT management that describes a commitment between the technology administrator, the one providing the service, and a client.	Overview of Syntax
sizeof()	Unary operation that queries the size of an object and delivers its size in bytes.	Unary Operators
Software Development Kit(SDK)	A set of tools used for developing applications provided by hardware and software providers.	Mac IDE Installation

| **Statements** | General term to describe the beginning line of code with specific instructions that the compiler recognizes outside of functions. How these are highlighted in language syntax environments depend on the typeof the statement and the | Overview of Syntax |

Term	Definition	See Also
	conventions of the programming environment.	
String Array	An orderly arrangement of characters where each character of the string is indexed in its own numerical location.	String Indexes and Arrays
Strings	A computer programming data type that represents a sequence of characters, either as a literal constant or as some kind of variable.	Advanced Strings
switch () Statement	Multibranch statement used to execute different code blocks based on the value of an evaluated expression	Loops

Ternary Operator	Classification of operators that accept more than 2 operands, or conditional operators with several arguments.	Ternary Operator
Text Editor	Program that enables editing of the code.	Chapter 1
Unary Operator	Classification of operators that	Unary Operator

	execute with a single operand.	
Variables	A concept borrowed from mathematics to describe a symbolic value who's associated value can be changed and operated upon. Variables are used to control a program through operational functions.	Chapter 3
while() Loop	Entry controlled loop that tests a single condition and loops a block of code until the condition is met.	Loops

Xcode	A free IDE software development suite for the macOS. This IDE has utilities for developing C++ based programs for MacOS oriented operating systems like tvOS for Apple TV, watchOS for Apple watches, and iPadOS for iPad tablets.	Mac Installation	IDE

Printed in the USA
CPSIA information can be obtained
at www.ICGtesting.com
CBHW071943051224
18487CB00047B/772